Sir W. Martin

Inquiries Concerning the Structure of the Semitic Languages

Part I.

Sir W. Martin

Inquiries Concerning the Structure of the Semitic Languages
Part I.

ISBN/EAN: 9783337062934

Printed in Europe, USA, Canada, Australia, Japan

Cover: Foto ©Thomas Meinert / pixelio.de

More available books at **www.hansebooks.com**

INQUIRIES

CONCERNING THE STRUCTURE

OF THE

SEMITIC LANGUAGES.

PART I.

BY

SIR W.ᵛ MARTIN, D.C.L..

E PUR SI MUOVE

WILLIAMS AND NORGATE,

14, HENRIETTA STREET, COVENT GARDEN, LONDON;
AND 20, SOUTH FREDERICK STREET, EDINBURGH.

1876.

IN MEMORY OF

JOHN COLERIDGE PATTESON,

MISSIONARY BISHOP IN MELANESIA,

WHO LAID DOWN HIS LIFE FOR HIS BRETHREN

20th September, 1871.

INDEX.

THE HEBREW VERB.

ERRATUM.

Page 16, line 7.   For *IMPERFECT* read *PERFECT*.

THE HEBREW VERB.

CHAPTER I.

INTRODUCTION.

1. Ever since the revival of learning in Western Europe, the structure of the Hebrew language has been a cause of perplexity to scholars.

In the middle of the last century, Bishop Lowth, in his *Lectures on the Sacred Poetry of the Hebrews,* having occasion to notice one of the chief difficulties of the subject, complained that interpreters of the Hebrew text, in their endeavours to escape from that difficulty, were driven to translate according to their own apprehension of the meaning rather than according to laws of Grammar, or any fixed principles. Writers on Grammar, he said, did indeed note the fact, but were unwilling to confess their inability to explain it: they attempted to hide their ignorance under a veil of technical terms. He could not believe that those unexplained variations of structure were introduced at random; on the contrary, it was beyond doubt that they had in them some special force and fitness.

1

It was not to be wondered at, that many of them appeared to us now intricate and obscure, considering the remote antiquity of the Hebrew language.[*]

2. The difficulties, to which Bishop Lowth referred, lay deep in the structure of the language. They concerned, chiefly, points on which, most of all, correctness of interpretation depends; namely, the power of the so-called Tenses of the Hebrew verb. The grammatical forms, to which this name was given in the days of Bishop Lowth, are two in number. They resemble tenses properly so called, in so far as they express action or condition, and as they combine with the root, which indicates that action or condition, certain prefixes and suffixes which indicate persons. It was natural that scholars, who were familiar with the languages of the West only, and derived thence their notions of grammar, should conceive they found in them the natural and typical structure of language in general; and should believe that these Hebrew forms, which so far resembled the tenses of those languages, resembled them further in that point from which the notion and name of tense were derived. As the notion of time, as past, present, or future, is inwrought into the very substance of the *tense*, so it was assumed that these forms carried in them the notion of time also. Accordingly, one of these forms was regarded as a Past Tense; the other, as a Future. The Present time was held to be sufficiently indicated in other ways.

[*] The passage, of which the substance is given above, occurs in Prælect. xv. " *Si adeamus Interpretes*," etc.

3. This theory had been long accepted: yet there were many obvious cases which it was inadequate to explain. In narratives of past events, the Hebrew use is to tell, one by one, acts or events in the order in which they occurred. Now the form ordinarily employed in such narratives for specifying each act or event was seen to be the form which it had been agreed to call the Future Tense. The events so narrated in due sequence were of course coupled by a conjunction, commonly rendered in the English Version by *and*. The original theory accordingly received an amendment or supplement. It was laid down that the conjunction had in such cases a special power of converting the Future Tense into a Past. A like difficulty presented itself in cases where the so-called Past Tense, with a conjunction prefixed, was used in passages where it was impossible to treat it as really indicating a past time. Here too a conversive power was conceived to belong to the conjunction.

It is a strong objection to this theory that no such use as that which is supposed has been found to exist in any of the other Semitic dialects, notwithstanding the close resemblance of those dialects to one another; nor in any other language.

It is a further objection that the supposed conversion is unnecessary and superfluous, even according to the principles of the supporters of this theory; for they assert that the language contains a proper Past Tense and a proper Future Tense. Why resort to these devices for converting a Future into a Past, a Past into a Future, when, as they assert, direct expressions for the Past and the Future already exist ?

After all, it was found necessary to admit that in certain cases the rule of conversion does not apply.

With all these qualifications, the theory, as above stated, is found in many cases insufficient, as is shown by the frequent instances in which the English translators of the Old Testament have departed from it.

4. Professor D. Michaelis, of Göttingen, in his *Annotations upon Bishop Lowth's Lectures*, indicated the error into which the grammarians had fallen. They had been misled by conceiving the structure of the Semitic verb to be completely similar to that of the verb in the languages with which they were conversant. He discerned that in the Hebrew the forms commonly called Tenses do in fact express no time, and that each of those forms is in fact used in reference sometimes to past time, sometimes to present or to future.

About the beginning of this century, Professor Jahn, of Vienna, in his *Grammatica Linguæ Hebrææ*, expounded this view, and in conformity with it abandoned the old technical names of the so-called Tenses. The forms, which had been formerly called Past and Future, he named First and Second Aorists. The general principle of the new theory he stated in the following words :

" Aoristus primus sistit *rem perfectam, jam præsentem, jam præteritam, jam futuram.*"

" Aoristus secundus sistit rem *imperfectam,* jam præsentem, jam præteritam, jam futuram."

In accordance with this view, later writers on Hebrew Grammar have named the two forms *Perfect* and *Imperfect.*

It is to be noticed also that writers of authority on the cognate dialect of Arabia now recognize the same principle as prevailing in that dialect, and adopt the same terms to designate the two corresponding forms of the Arabic verb. "The temporal forms of the Arabic verb (says Professor Wright) are but two in number; the one expressing a *finished* act, one that is done and completed in relation to other acts (the *Perfect*); the other, an *unfinished* act, one that is just commencing or in progress (the *Imperfect*). A Semitic Perfect or Imperfect has, in and of itself, no reference to the temporal relations of the speaker." (*Grammar of the Arabic Language,* vol. i. s. 77.)

5. Another important advance towards a true theory of Hebrew Grammar was made about the same time by Professor Heinrich Ewald, of Göttingen. He appears to have been the first to discern the correspondence of the two conjunctions, which in our Authorized Version are indifferently rendered by our English *and*, with the two conjunctions which in Arabic appear as *wa* and *fa :* the former expressing *connexion*, the latter indicating *sequence* or *consequence.* Ewald's view is now generally received.

6. Notwithstanding the progress thus made, we find that our best treatises on Hebrew Grammar do not furnish any clear and consistent theory. We find, for instance, the verbal forms still named the Past Tense and the Future Tense, whilst it is admitted that these tenses mark also all other times. We still read of the Future with Vau

Conversive; yet the use of that construction is described as being that of marking an advance or progress in the events related. Thus the old and the new are combined, though they cannot be harmonized. Old terms are retained, though the theory to which those terms were fitted is abandoned; and the new theory is adopted, apart from the new terms, which alone fitly express it.

As to the unsatisfactory state of Semitic scholarship at this time, it will be sufficient to cite the testimony of Bishop Ellicott:

"It would certainly seem that, much as has of late been done for the study of the Hebrew language, especially in Germany, there is still room for a more scientific development of many of the laws by which that ancient language appears to be governed. There is even now (as a reference to any of the more recent commentaries on the books of the Old Testament will clearly show) less linguistic precision, less mastery of details, less recognition of those bye-laws which in every language, but especially in the Semitic, so much regulate special interpretations—less, in a word, of scholarship, as distinguished from learning, than we might have expected from the corresponding advances in the Greek language."—(*Aids to Faith*, p. 456.)

7. This state of things renders it highly desirable that some effort be made to ascertain and to define accurately the principles and the rules by which the structure of the Hebrew language is regulated. The Scriptures of the Old Testament are at this time subjected to a searching criticism: a revision of the Authorized Version is actually

in hand : yet the best security against error appears to be wanting.

8. However needful some work of this kind may be, it may well seem strange that this task should be undertaken by persons far distant from the centres of European learning, and without the advantage of personal communication with living teachers of highest authority. It may appear to be a somewhat presumptuous attempt to enter upon a field which might have been more fitly left to others. It may be well, therefore, to state the circumstances under which this work was commenced.

The two friends, the result of whose inquiries on this subject is given in this volume, had acquired some knowledge of the Semitic tongues before they entered on the study of the dialects of the Southern Pacific. They were struck, as earlier students had been, by certain points of resemblance between the two groups : not a resemblance in words, or such as would indicate any affinity in the roots of the languages, but rather one which lies in the structure of speech, in the forms of thought, and which seems to show that the two groups belong to a similar stage in the growth of language. In particular it was noticed that in these languages forms of the verb exist, which convey the notion of action or condition, and nothing more ; the time to which the action or condition belonged being left to be gathered from the context, or from the circumstances under which the words are spoken. Here, then, was a grammatical form, the existence of which had been divined by European students of Hebrew, but of which no actual instance had been known to the learned men of Western Europe.

Further, it was obvious that even the rudest of the known languages of the ocean, however simple in structure or deficient in flexion, do yet suffice to convey from man to man with reasonable accuracy those notions of time, of position, connexion, or relation, without which speech would fail of its end. There is always present some device of structure, or of mere collocation, which, being understood alike by speaker and hearer, excludes doubt or misunderstanding as to these points. It was hard to think that the Hebrew tongue did not possess some adequate means of conveying thought with more of precision than had been apparent to our grammarians.

Accordingly we set ourselves to examine carefully the Hebrew documents, endeavouring to ascertain, by a comparison of passages, the rules by which the use of the several forms of the Hebrew verb was controlled, and to define, so far as might be practicable, the more minute rules by which the speakers of the language were guided in other respects.

The work went on smoothly as long as my friend shared in it. His wide knowledge corroborated what had been inferred from a narrower field, and furnished many new suggestions. Amid many cares, his interest in this undertaking—his conviction that it would in due time yield fruit—never faltered. To his co-operation and encouragement whilst he lived, and since his departure to the re-

membrance of his urgent words, it is due that the inquiry
has been carried thus far. If time and strength be given,
other researches in the same field may be brought to completion.

———————

Throughout the following pages, the letters and vowel-
points of the Hebrew are replaced by characters and
marks more familiar to our eyes.

Alef is not expressed otherwise than by the vowel of
which it is the vehicle.

Beth, Peh and Tau, with *dagesh*, are represented by
b, p, t; without *dagesh*, by v, f, θ:

The sibilants *Samech, Tsade, Sin* and *Shin*, by s, ṣ, ś, *s*
italic.

The remaining letters, following the order of the
Hebrew Alphabet, are represented by g, d, h, w, z, χ,
t italic, y, k, l, m, n, ʻ, *k* italic, r:

The moveable *Sheva* and its Compounds, by ĕ, ă, and ŏ.

CHAPTER II.

GENERAL RULES.

The Rules set forth in this chapter are deduced from a careful examination of the Hebrew text. The examples here given as illustrating the Rules have been chiefly taken from the Historical Books as they stand in the Hebrew Canon, beginning with Genesis and ending with the Second Book of Kings. Though the style of these books is for the greater part of the historical or narrative kind, yet there is a large admixture of other elements. There are numerous examples of the ordinary speech of the Hebrew people intermingled with the more solemn discourses of the lawgiver and the prophet, and with songs of triumph and devotion. To these books belong two especial advantages for our purpose: the context is generally sufficiently clear to aid the reader in determining the true rendering; and there are few passages as to which prepossessions might interfere with the fairness of our induction. Occasionally, examples have been added from the Psalms and the Book of Proverbs.

1. The Forms of the Hebrew verb, which are here called

Imperfect and *Perfect*, are not tenses in the proper sense, *i.e.* the notion of time as past, present or future, is not inherent in the Form. They note only actions or conditions and the persons of whom such actions or conditions are predicated. They predicate a certain state of a certain subject, and no more.

The *time* to which the action or condition, expressed by the form, belongs in each case, is to be gathered from the context. The present time is understood, if none other is suggested by the context. The difference between the two Forms is not then any difference in time, but a difference in the way of conceiving the action or condition. The Forms then may be accurately described as *moods* indicating modes of thought, rather than as tenses. These moods taken in connexion with indications of time supplied by the context, and so having their generality limited and restricted, become equivalent to our tenses. Viewed as moods, they differ from each other much in the same way as *becoming* from *being*, as *motion* from *rest*, as *progress* from *completion*.

IMPERFECT.

2. The *Imperfect* is used, in *independent* sentences or clauses, to express acts or events which are regarded as transitory or incomplete, commencing at some particular point of time, or continuing during some interval of time, past, present or future. It may be (*a*) a single act: or (*b*) a recurring act: or (*c*) an act expected to

occur in a certain state of things whenever that may arise ; or (*d*) an act dependent on other acts, hypothetical, or contingent. This Form is used also (*e*) after words of prohibition or deprecation.

EXAMPLES.

a. Judges xix. 16, 17, "There came an old man from his work, and he *saw* a wayfaring man in the street of the city. And the old man said, *Whither goest thou ?* and *whence comest thou ?*" (tēlēk—tāvō).

I. Samuel xxviii. 16. "Wherefore then *dost thou ask of* me ?" (tisālēnī).

Gen. xv. 13. "Thy seed *shall be* a stranger in a land that is not theirs" (yihyeh). The words "thy seed" suggest a future time, being addressed to a man who at the time has no child.

Exod. ix. 5. "To-morrow the Lord *shall do* this thing" (ya'aśeh).

b. Deut. iii. 9, E.V. "Hermon the Sidonians *call* Sirion" (yiḳrĕū), *i.e.* they call it so from time to time whenever they have occasion to speak of it.

I. Kings v. 25, Heb. (v. 11, E.V.). "Thus gave Solomon to Hiram year by year" (yittēn).

Numb. xi. 5, E.V. "We remember the fish which we *did eat* in Egypt freely" (nōkal). The past time is supplied by the words "in Egypt." The eating was an act recurring from time to time—at meal-times, or when hunger returned.

c. Prov. xi. 4. "Riches *profit not* in the day of wrath (*i.e.* whenever wrath falleth upon man) ; but righteousness *delivereth* from death (*i.e.* delivereth whenever death is imminent)" (lo-yōᵈl—taṣṣīl).

d. Thus the Imperfect is regularly used after the words *im* (if), *pen* (lest), *lĕ-ma an* (to the intent), *ki* (in case).

e. "Thou shalt not steal" (lō tignōv). "Fear thou not" (al-tīrā).

PERFECT.

3. The *Perfect* is used, in *independent* sentences or clauses, to express (*a*) states, conditions or relations which are regarded as complete and abiding, belonging to no particular point or interval of time; (*b*) states of the human mind and feelings, habits or customs, course of life; (*c*) offices, functions, or permanent relations; (*d*) facts regarded as complete, and entirely past; (*e*) facts regarded as absolutely certain to happen.

EXAMPLES.

a. Psalm civ. 1. "O Lord, Thou *art* very *great*. Thou *art clothed* with honour and majesty" (gādaltā—lāvāstā).

b. Psalm cxix. 113, 114. "*I hate* vain thoughts, but Thy law do *I love*. *I hope* in thy word" (śānēθī—āhavtī —yiχālti).

Ps. i. 1. "Blessed is the man that *walketh* not in the counsel of the ungodly, nor *standeth* in the way of sinners, nor *sitteth* in the seat of the scornful" (lō hālak—ᵃmad —yāsav).

I. Sam. ii. 13, 14. "The priest's custom with the people was—when any man offered sacrifice, the priest's servants *came* with a flesh-hook, and *he struck* it into the pan" (vā—hikkāh).

c. II. Kings ix. 13. "Then they hasted, and blew with a trumpet, saying, Jehu *is king*" (mālak).

Deut. viii. 19, E. V. "I testify (am a witness) against you this day" (haᴄidōθī).

d. I. Sam. vii. 12, E. V. "Hitherto hath the Lord helped us" (ᴄazārānū).

Deut. v. 2-4. "The Lord *made a covenant* with us in Horeb" (kāraθ—bĕrīθ). "The Lord *talked* with you, in the mount" (dibber).

In these verses a past time is indicated by referring to Horeb and to the mount.

Joshua xxiv. 2, E. V. "Your fathers *dwelt* on the other side of the flood in old time" (yāsĕvū).

e. I. Sam. ii. 31. "Behold the days come that I will *cut* off thine arm, and the arm of thy father's house, that there shall not be an old man in thy house" (gādaᴄti).

I. Kings xiii. 2. "O altar, altar, thus saith the Lord; Behold, a child shall *be born* unto the house of David, Josiah by name; and upon thee shall *he offer*" (nōlād—wĕ-zāvaχ).

4. In order to make the meaning and effect of these two forms of the Verb more manifest, it is desirable to compare the uses of the two forms in cases where both belong to the same root.

For example, compare the Imperfect and Perfect of the root *bā*, in Judges xix. 16, 17; and in Gen. xvi. 8. In the former passage the wayfaring man is moving on from one place to another, one action still continuing. So the Imperfect is used (tēlēk—tāvō). Whereas in Gen. xvi. 8, Hagar is resting by a fountain. One action is complete; another has to begin. The Perfect is used of the former; the Imperfect of the latter (vā𝜃—tēlēkī).

So likewise as to the root *āmar.*

In II. Kings xx. there are narrated two conversations between King Hezekiah and the prophet Isaiah: one in vv. 8-10; and the other in vv. 14-19. In both cases the narrative takes the ordinary shape: the words of each speaker being given in their due order, and the Imperfect being used. But in the preceding chapter we find that certain persons were sent to deliver a message from the king to the prophet: "And they said unto him, *Thus saith Hezekiah*" (v. 3). Here the Perfect is used. The act of speaking is not thought of, but only the fact that these are words which express the mind of the king, a royal and weighty message. So the prophet answers (v. 6), "Thus shall ye say to your master, *Thus saith the Lord,*" using also on his part the Perfect, meaning "This is the Divine message in answer to that of the king.

So as to the verb shāfat to *judge.*

Exod. xviii. 25-26, *lit.* "Then Moses chooses able men. And *they judge* the people at *all times.* The hard causes *they bring unto* Moses, but every small matter *they judge* themselves" (shāfĕtū—yĕvīūn—yishpūtū). Here Moses appoints certain men, and these men, being so appointed, are judges, and habitually exercise the function of judges.

This custom or function is expressed by the Perfect (wĕ-shāfĕ*tū*). In the course of this function, from time to time they carry some causes to Moses, the others they settle. If a cause be difficult, they carry it to Moses; if plain, they settle it themselves. These last acts are therefore properly expressed by an Imperfect.

SUBJOINED IMPERFECT.

5. It is sometimes needful to enumerate several successive acts which, taken together, make up one proceeding or transaction, or are subordinate to one end or purpose. In such cases all the verbs subsequent to the first are in the Perfect, *wĕ* being prefixed to each Perfect. The first verb, taken with the context, having sufficiently shown the nature and. circumstances of the transaction and the time thereof, all that remains is to designate the several steps in their order, and to indicate the close connexion of each step with the steps preceding. This is done by recurring to the Perfect, which, being the more simple and radical form of the Verb, is fitly used to express the action of the Verb *per se*. Such Perfects are hereafter spoken of as *subjoined* Perfects.

Such an enumeration may form part of (*a*) a command, (*b*) a law, (*c*) a narrative, (*d*) a question, or (*e*) a dependent or hypothetical clause.

It is not necessary in these cases that the subjects or agents of the several verbs so put in the Perfect remain so throughout. They may be varied without affecting the operation of the rule.

Sometimes, in enumerating the parts of the transaction itself, it is found convenient to mention some secondary or collateral act appertaining to the transaction. For this purpose, the sequence of Perfects is interrupted, and a parenthesis inserted; in such case, the *wĕ* which introduces the parenthesis is coupled, not with the verb, but with a noun or pronoun, and the verb is put in the Imperfect. This Imperfect, being now the verb of a direct and independent clause and relating to a transaction yet unbegun, is to be taken as a future.

EXAMPLES.

a. Levit. xviii. 2. "Speak unto the children of Israel, *and say* unto them" (dabbēr—wĕ-āmartā).

Genesis xxvii. 43, 44. "*Flee thou* to Laban—*and tarry* with him" (bĕraχ-lĕ-kā—wĕ-yasavtā).

Judges vi. 25, 26, *lit.* "*Take* thy father's bullock and *throw down* the altar of Baal—(and the grove that is by it thou shalt cut down)—and *build* an altar unto the Lord, and *take* the second bullock and *offer* a burnt sacrifice" (ḳaχ—wĕ-hārástā—(wĕ-eθ-hā-ăserāh—tikroθ)—ū-vanīθa —wĕ-lākaχtā—wĕ-ha‘alīθā).

Here the object directly contemplated is the destruction of the idol-altar, and the substitution of an altar unto the Lord, and the offering of a sacrifice thereon. In carrying out this purpose, there is an opportunity for further dishonouring the idol-worship, and thereby providing wood for the sacrifice. This, being a secondary and subordinate part of the transaction, is placed in a parenthesis.

Exodus xl. 2-13. "On the first day of the first month

shalt thou set up the tabernacle—and thou shalt *put therein*
the ark—and *cover* the ark—and thou shalt *bring in* the
table and *set in order*—" (tākīm—wĕ-śamtā—wĕ-sakkōθā
—wĕ-hēvēθā—wĕ-ʿāraktā, etc.).

This example, on account of its length, is not here set
fully out. It extends from v. 2 to v. 13.

The acts here commanded had for their object the completion on one day of all the preparations needful in order
to the carrying out of the sacrificial system. All were
subordinate to that one end. Accordingly every step
after the first is indicated by a Perfect with *wĕ* prefixed.

b. Leviticus i. 3-9. "He *shall offer it* at the door of the
tabernacle, and he shall *put* his hand upon the head of
the burnt-offering, and it shall *be accepted.* And he shall
kill the bullock, and the priests shall *bring* the blood and
sprinkle the blood round about upon the altar, and he shall
flay the burnt-offering and *cut it into pieces,* and the sons of
Aaron *shall put fire* upon the altar and *lay* the wood *in
order.* And the priests *shall lay* the parts *in order* upon
the wood, (but *his inwards*—shall *he wash* in water) and
the priest shall *burn* all upon the altar" (yakrīv—wĕ-
sāmak—wĕ-niṣrāh—wĕ-sāχat—wĕ-hikrīvū—wĕ-zārekū
— wĕ-hifsīt — wĕ-nittaχ — wĕ-nāθĕnū — wĕ-ʿārĕkū —
wĕ-ʿārĕkū (wĕ-kirb-ō—yirχaṣ) wĕ-hīktīr).

In this example a parenthesis is introduced relating to
a special act which the priest is to perform in reference
not to the whole offering, but to one part only of it.

c. Genesis ii. 6. "There *went up a* mist and *watered*
the ground " (ēd yaʿăleh—wĕ-hiskāh).

Genesis xl. 19. "Within three days shall Pharaoh *lift up thine* head, and shall *hang* thee—and the birds shall *eat* thy flesh" (yiśśā P.—wĕ-θālāh—wĕ-ākal).

Joshua xv. 2-4. "Their south border *was* from the shore of the salt sea, and it *went out* to the south side to M. and *passed* along to Z. and *ascended* up unto K. and *passed along* to H. and *went up* to A. and *fetched a compass* to Ka : it *passed* towards A. and *went out* unto the river of Egypt, and the goings out *were* at the sea" (wa-ihī—wĕ-yāṣū—wĕ-ʿāvar — wĕ-ʿālāh— wĕ-ʿāvar— wĕ-ʿālāh — wĕ-nāsav — wĕ-ʿāvar—wĕ-yāṣū—wĕ-hāyāh).

Here one continuous boundary line is traced from spot to spot through its whole length.

d. Exod. ii. 7. "Shall I *go and call* to thee a nurse of the Hebrew women ?" (ha-ēlēk—wĕ-kūraθī ?).

e. Deut. viii. 1. "All the commandments shall ye observe to do, that ye may *live* and *multiply* and *go in* and possess the land" (lĕ-maʿan tiχyūn ū-rĕvīθem ū-vāθem w-īrishtem).

Genesis xxviii. 20, 21. "If God will *be* with me, and will *keep* me in the way that I go, and *will give* me bread to eat and raiment to put on, and I *come again* to my father's house, then," etc. (im yihyeh—ū-sĕmārānī-wĕ-nāθan—wĕ-savtī).

It is scarcely necessary to remark that the foregoing examples under this rule are sufficient of themselves to show that a notion of past time cannot be inherent in the Perfect as such.

PARTICLE OF CONNEXION.

6. The particle *we*, commonly rendered by *and*, in its ordinary use connects objects present at the same time, or acts which are either simultaneous or at least closely connected with one another.

This particle does not indicate any change of time. It has in itself no reference to time. It is true that, in an enumeration of acts forming several parts of one transaction, the several stages do belong to different points of time. This however is not shown by the particle, but rather by the nature of the steps or stages, of which each one as it comes into existence shows the before-mentioned steps or stages to have been completed.

7. In order to express the close connexion of two acts, or the immediate dependence of one act upon another, the dependent act is put in the Imperfect, *wĕ* being prefixed immediately to the Imperfect.

In sentences of this class the modes of connexion or dependence are various, each of which has in English its appropriate form of expression. In Hebrew the one method, by the use of *wĕ* prefixed to the Imperfect, is made to serve all these purposes. Occasionally other forms of speech are resorted to, but as a general rule this form is employed. The nature of the acts indicated by the verbs; the relation between the persons who are the subjects or agents of the verbs ; these and other points mentioned or suggested by the context supply a sufficient guide to the meaning.

a. In some cases, the connexion is so close that the dependent act is involved in the fact or supposition stated in
the former clause.

Numb. xxiii. 19. "God is not a man *that he should lie,*
neither a son of man *that he should repent*" (w-ĭkazzēv—
wĕ-yiθnĕχām).

I. Samuel xii. 3. "Of whose hand have I received any
bribe *to blind* mine eyes therewith ? " (wĕ-ʿalīm).

I. Kings xxii. 7, E. V. "Is there not here a prophet of
the Lord besides, *that we may inquire* of him ? " (wĕ-
nidrēsāh), *i.e.* if there be such a prophet, of course we
shall inquire of him.

Psalm li. 18. "Thou desirest not sacrifice, else would I
give it" (wĕ-ettēnāh).

b. In others, the dependent verb expresses the purport
and object of the act expressed by the verb in the former
clause.

Exodus vi. 11. "*Speak* unto Pharaoh *that he let* the
children of Israel *go*" (w-ĭsallaχ).

Exodus x. 17, E.V. "Entreat the Lord, *that he take away*
from me this death" (wĕ-yāsēr).

Exodus ii. 7. "Then said his sister to *Pharaoh's* daughter,
Shall I go and call to thee a nurse of the Hebrew *women,
that she may nurse* the child for thee" (wĕ-θēnik).

I. Kings xiii. 33, E. V. "Whosoever would, Jeroboam
consecrated him *that he might become* one of the priests of
the high places" (w-ĭhī).

c. In other cases a command or prayer is followed by a

clause expressing a result of such command being obeyed or prayer granted.

Gen. xii. 1, 2. "Get thee out of thy country, *and I will make of thee* a great nation " (wĕ-e₍ĕś-kā).

Psalm cxix. 144. " Give me understanding *and I shall live*" (wĕ-eχyeh).

I. Sam. vii. 3. "Prepare your hearts unto the Lord and serve Him only: and He *will deliver* you" (wĕ-yaṣṣēl).

8. When a statement of a *condition or supposition* is followed by a statement of some *result* to follow closely upon the fulfilment of that condition, the verb which expresses the result is in the Perfect form, and is preceded by *wĕ*. The result necessarily belongs to the future time at which the specified condition shall be fulfilled.

EXAMPLES.

Genesis xxviii. 20, 21. "If God will be with me and will keep me and will give me bread to eat, etc., *then shall the Lord be* my God" (wĕ-hāyāh).

Numbers xxvii. 8. "If a man die and have no son, *then ye shall cause* his inheritance *to pass* unto his daughter" (wĕ-ha₍āvartem).

The same construction recurs in vv. 9, 10, 11.

In the following and similar cases, the supposition is not put in express words, but clearly implied.

Genesis xviii. 25. "That be far from Thee to do after this manner, to slay the righteous with the wicked. (If Thou do so), *then happeneth* (this state of things), as the righteous, so the wicked" (wĕ-hāyāh).

Exodus xxxiii. 16. " Wherein shall it be known that I

and thy people have found grace in thy sight? Is it not in that Thou goest with us? (If Thou so goest with us), then *are we separated* from all the people upon the face of the earth" (wĕ-niflīnū).

II. Sam. xiv. 7. "They said, Deliver him that smote his brother that we may kill him, *and so* (*i.e.* if they kill him) *they shall quench* my coal which is left" (wĕ-kibbū).

PARTICLE OF SEQUENCE.

9. Whenever past events are narrated in due order, the sequence is indicated by prefixing the conjunction *wa* to the several verbs which express those events, each verb being put in the Imperfect form. The *wa* in every such case marks a new time, the commencement of a new act or event. It shows that the act expressed by the verb to which it is prefixed is later in time than the act indicated by the last preceding verb having *wa* similarly prefixed. It expresses *sequence*, and nothing more: the interval between the acts may be of the shortest or the longest.

The *wa* should be understood as equivalent to *after that, thereupon, so, then.*

Of this structure, examples are found in every part of the historical books. It should be noticed that the first letter of the Imperfect following the *wa* is doubled, *e.g.* wai-yōmer—wat-tōmer.

The following examples will show clearly the use of this particle as contrasted with the particle of connexion.

I. Kings i. 33–35. "The king said unto them, Take with you the servants of your lord, and *cause Solomon to ride* upon my own mule, and *bring him down* to Gihon : And let Zadok *anoint* him there king over Israel, and *blow ye* with the trumpet, and *say*, God save the king" (wĕ-hirkavtem—wĕ-hōradtem—ū-māsaχ—ū-θĕkaᵈtem).

Ib. 38, 39. "So Zadok and Nathan went down and *caused* Solomon to ride upon king David's mule, and brought him to Gihon. And Zadok *anointed* Solomon, and *they blew* the trumpet, and all the people *said*, God save king Solomon" (wai-yarkīvū — wai-yōlikū — wai-yimsaχ—wai-yiθkĕᵈū—wai-yōmĕrū).

In I. Sam. ix. 27, the Imperfect of the verb ᵈāvar occurs twice : once with the *wĕ*, the second time with the *wa* prefixed. Samuel said to Saul, "Speak to the servant *that he pass on*" (wĕ-yaᵈāvōr). "*Then* the servant *passed on*" (wai-yaᵈāvor).

10. The use of this idiom is not confined to narratives of a strictly historical kind. It extends to narratives of every kind : to Jotham's similitude (Judges ix. 8—15); to Nathan's parable (II. Sam. xii. 1—4); as well as to a narrative given by a prophet of matters which passed before him in vision (I. Kings xxii. 19—23).

It is used also for the purpose of setting forth facts, not as occurring at a specified time, but as recurring from time to time whenever the like circumstances recur ; and that not only in respect of physical sequences or consequences, but also in respect of those of a moral kind.

Thus Proverbs xi. 2 : When pride is come, *then cometh* shame" (wai-yāvō).

11. In poetry, the *wa* of sequence may be omitted, and

the Imperfect alone used : *e.g.* Exodus xv. 12. "Thou stretchedst out thy right hand, the earth swallowed them" (tivlā⸴ēmū).

BREACH OF SEQUENCE.

12. When it is found necessary to interrupt the orderly course of a narrative for the purpose of mentioning some fact contemporaneous with some fact already narrated, or which may serve to explain or to enlarge upon something previously stated, the *breach in the sequence* of the narrative is indicated by a very simple device. The structure is suddenly changed : the *wa* and its Imperfect disappear. The new sentence begins with *wĕ*, but this *wĕ* is prefixed, not to the leading verb, but to a noun or pronoun ; and the leading verb of the new sentence is put in the Perfect.

EXAMPLES.

Judges iii. 25, 26. "Therefore *they tarried* till they were ashamed—then *they took* their key, and *opened* the door. *But* Ehud *escaped* while they tarried" (wai-yāχīlū—wai-yikχū—wai-yiftaχū—wĕ-Ehūd nimla*t*).

Numbers xxiv. 25. "Then Balaam *rose up* and *went* and *returned* to his place, *and Balak* also *went* his way" (wai-yāḳōm—wai-yēlek—wai-yāshōv—wĕ-gam Bālak—hālak). That is to say, the journey of Balak took place not after that of Balaam, but during the same time.

Judges ix. 51—54. "Then *went* Abimelech to Thebez, and encamped against Thebez, and *took* it. (*But there was a strong tower* within the city) and thither *fled* all the men and women, and *shut it to* them and *gat them up* to the top. And Abimelech *came* unto the tower " (wai-yēlek—wai-yiχan—wai-yilkĕdāh (ū-migdal ɪ̇ōz hāyāh—)—wai-yānusū—wai-yisgĕrū—wai-yaɪ̇alū—wai-yāvō).

I. Samuel ix. 14, 15. "*And they went up* Saul and the servant into the city, and when they were come into the city, behold, Samuel came out. Now the Lord *had told* Samuel a day before Saul came, saying," etc. (wai-yaɪ̇alū—wĕ-Y. gālāh).

II. Samuel xviii. 18. " Now Absalom in his life-time *had taken* and reared up for himself a pillar " (wĕ-Absalom lāḵaχ).

13. It has already been stated that *wa*, as a Particle of Sequence, occurs before the Imperfect Form only. But there are apparent exceptions—that is to say, there are cases in which *wa* is found before other parts of the verb, and even before nouns. In all such instances, the *wa* is a disguised form of the particle *wĕ*. For it is a rule of the language that *wĕ* (and all other similar particles, such as *bĕ*, *lĕ*, etc.) must undergo this change, when they stand immediately before a word beginning with Alef or any aspirated letter. Then the *wĕ* becomes *wa*, and in like manner *bĕ* and *lĕ* become *ba* and *la*. In certain cases they even become *wā*, *bā*, and *lā*.

By the operation of this rule, the Particle of Sequence becomes subject to one change : it becomes *wā* before the 1st person singular of the Imperfect which begins with Alef. Thus, in I. Sam. xiii. 12, we observe three instances of this change in one verse : wā-ōmar—wā-eθappak—

wā-a.āleh. But these are matters of euphony, not
of grammar, and do not further concern us in this
inquiry.

14. It is not meant to be asserted that the rule as to
this Particle of Sequence is so rigidly observed as never
to be broken—at least, apparently. It is not maintained
that every sentence commencing with the *wa* and the
Imperfect does in fact indicate a time later than every
similar sentence which occurs before it in the text. The
Hebrew writers used the freedom of a simple and in-
artificial style ; and in the writings of which the volume
of Scripture is composed, proceeding from many hands
and having passed through many generations, some irregularities are to be expected. There are cases where the
narrator returns to a prior point in his narrative, as at
Genesis v. 24, where some of the words of verse 22 are
repeated : and again at Judges ii..6, where the very words
of Joshua xxiv. 28 are repeated, with some addition : and
at Judges ii. 7, where the words of Joshua xxiv. 31 are
repeated in like manner. Sometimes the writer appears
to go back to a point already reached and passed, for the
purpose of supplying details not yet stated, *e.g.* II. Sam.
iv. 5—7. Sometimes the order appears to be thrown
wrong by way of parenthesis or a later insertion, as in the
passage Joshua iv. 11—18. In I. Kings xiii. 12 (wai-
yirū), where the rendering " had seen " is untenable, the
LXX. must have read (wai-yarū).

But irregularities of this kind are not of such a kind
or so numerous as to throw any doubt upon the rule ;

which, with these exceptions and some few others of the like kind, is observed throughout the historical books.

CONCURRENT FACTS.

15. In order to indicate that two states or events are *concurrent, or immediately connected,* the clauses expressing the two are put in the same grammatical form, and placed side by side.

EXAMPLES.

Exodus xvi. 21. "As the sun *waxed hot,* it (the manna) *melted* " (wĕ-χam—wĕ-nāmas).

I. Sam. ix. 17. "And as soon as Samuel *saw Saul,* the Lord *said* unto him" (ū-*S.* rāāh—wa-Y. ʿānāh-ū).

I. Kings xiv. 17. "As she came to the threshold, the child *died*" (hī bāāh—wĕ-han-naʿar mēθ).

Gen. xliv. 3. "As soon as the morning *was light,* the men were sent away " (hab-bōḳer ōr, wĕ-hā-anāsīm sullĕχū).

II. Sam. vi. 16. E.V. "And as the ark of the Lord came into the city, Michal looked down," *lit.* and it *came to pass* (this was the state of things). The ark was *come* into the city, and Michal *looked* down (wĕ-hāyāh—ārōn Y. bā—ū. M. niskĕfāh).

16. There are various passages in which the grammatical form remains the same as in the foregoing examples, but much more than mere concurrence of events is implied. In these cases the further meaning is suggested by a consideration of the relation subsisting between the person speaking and the person addressed.

Judges vii. 18, E. V. "When I blow with a trumpet, then blow ye the trumpets also." (*i.e.* "When I (your commander) blow, then it is your duty to blow also.") (wĕ-θāka·tī—ănōkī—u-θĕka·tem gam-attem).

II. Kings v. 6. sālaχtī — wa-āsaft-ō (*wa* instead of *we* before Alef). *Lit.* "I send Naaman unto thee, and thou recoverest him from his leprosy," *i.e.* "When I require thee to do this thing, it is thy business to do it." The superiority of the King of Syria at that time appears from verses 1, 2 and 6.

A similar construction is found at II. Kings x. 2, 3.

These examples appear to explain the structure of the passage in Deuteronomy xxx. 19. "Life and death I place before thy face — and thou choosest life." *i.e.* "When I, the lawgiver, set life and death before thee, then thou (as in duty bound) choosest life."

PRECATIVE FORM.

17. A *precative or optative sense* is given to the Imperfect by placing it at the commencement of the sentence, and placing the noun which expresses the subject or agent of the Imperfect immediately after it.

EXAMPLES.

Judges xi. 37. "Let *this thing* be *done*" (yē·āśeh—had-dāvūr haz-zeh).

Numbers vi. 24—26. "The Lord *bless thee*—the Lord *make his face to shine* upon thee—the Lord *lift up* the light of his countenance" (yĕvārek-kā Y.—yāer Y.—yiśśū Y.).

II. Kings xi. 12. "Long live the King" (yĕχī hammelek).

Judges xvi. 30. "Let *me die* with the Philistine" (tāmōθ nafs-ī).

Genesis xvi. 5. "The Lord judge between me and thee" (yispōt Y.).

There are, however, cases where the subject of the verb is put in the first place, the speaker seeming to pause upon it with an emphasis before he utters his prayer concerning it, *e.g.* Psalm cix. 6. "Set thou a wicked man over him —and *Satan—let him stand* at his right hand" (wĕ-Sātān —ya·ămōd).

After a verb in the Imperative or Precative form, the *second* person of the Imperfect is often used in a Precative sense.

EXAMPLES.

Psalm lxviii. 3. "Let *God arise,* let his enemies be scattered: As smoke is driven away, so *drive Thou them away*" (tindōf).

Proverbs vii. 1. "My son, *keep* my words, and *lay up* my commandments with thee" (semōr—tisfōn).

18. In I. Samuel xx. 16, there is a singular instance of a *Perfect* placed before a noun to express a prayer. "So Jonathan made a covenant with the house of David, saying, 'Let the Lord even require it at the hand of David's enemies,' *i.e.* require the due penalty for the evil which David's enemies are supposed to be doing at the time of uttering the prayer" (ū-vikkēs Y.). This may be compared with similar forms in Arabic, *e.g. tabāraka*

'llahu, which seem to be used for the purpose of expressing a pious wish for the continuance of some *existing state*
of things.

PARTICIPLE.

19. The *Participle* so-called resembles the Perfect inasmuch as it couples with some person or subject the action
or condition expressed by the root, without conveying in
itself any notion of time past, present, or future. It differs
from the Perfect inasmuch as it does not assert or predicate, but only describes. It is the *nomen agentis* or *nomen
patientis* of Arabic Grammars.

EXAMPLES.

Proverbs xx. 12. " The *hearing* ear, and the *seeing* eye,
the Lord hath made even both of them " (sōma* a*θ—rōāh),
i.e. the *ear*, which possesses the faculty of hearing, and
the *eye*, which possesses the faculty of seeing.

Prov. xx. 11. " It is naught, it is naught, saith the
buyer " (ha*k*-*k*ōneh).

Gen. i. 6. " Let there be a firmament—and let it be a
divider—between waters and waters " (mavdīl).

Exodus xx. 12 (Deut. v. 16). "The land which the
Lord giveth thee (*lit.* of which the Lord is *giver*)" (nōθēn).
This form seems to be intended to suggest as a motive
to obedience the relation subsisting (apart from all considerations of time) between the Author of the law and
his people. He who gives the law, and requires obedience
thereto from the dwellers in the land, is also the giver of
the land on which they dwell.

In the case of the Participle, as in the case of the Perfect, the notion of the time past, present, or future, to which the act or condition belongs, is to be gathered from the context.

Numbers xxxiii. 3, 4. "The children of Israel went out with a high hand in the sight of all the Egyptians: For the Egyptians *were burying* all their first-born" (mĕkabbĕrīm).

Joshua iii. 17. "And the priests that bare the ark—stood firm on dry ground—whilst all the Israelites *were passing* over" (wĕ-kol I. —ʿōvĕrīm).

HEBREW NARRATIVE.

20. In comparing the structure of the Verb in the Hebrew and in other Semitic languages with the structure of the Verb in the cultivated languages of the West, we are struck by the *fewness of the grammatical forms* employed by the former class; and we are apt to wonder, how so scanty an outfit was made to meet the requirements of human discourse. In considering this question, we confine ourselves to the case of narratives of past events.

The chief cause then seems to lie in the mental habits of the speakers of the language.

Our habit is to refer all the parts of every narrative to one fixed centre; namely, to the narrator himself in each case, however remote he may be in time from the facts he is narrating. From the time at which he speaks, or writes, he travels back in mind to the facts narrated. He not only indicates in the outset that the facts stated belong to the past time, but goes on repeating that indication with every new fact in the series narrated.

Moreover, we are apt in our written narratives to gather the events which we narrate into groups, each group having for its centre some person, from whose stand-point we look before and after. We not only indicate the place of that central figure as in the past, but upon every motive or remembrance, and even upon every hope or fear which we assign to him, we think it necessary to set a further mark showing that to us all is past.

The Hebrew narrator proceeds on a different plan. He begins by indicating once for all that he is about to speak of a past time. This he does either by expressly mentioning the past time to which his narrative belongs, or by naming some person, or event which his hearers know beforehand to belong to the past time.

21. By way of *Preface,* he sets forth the state of facts as existing at the time of the commencement of his intended narrative, so far as may be needed to make that narrative intelligible. These facts are viewed only as being the facts out of which the narrative takes its rise. The course of things by which those facts came into being, their relations in time to each other, these matters lie outside of the purpose and business of the narrator. The facts are viewed simply as co-existing at the outset of the narrative, and are therefore connected together by means of the ordinary conjunction *wĕ*. In these prefaces there is no dependence of the acts or conditions therein men-

tioned upon one another; the *wĕ* being prefixed in each case, not to a verb, but to a noun.

For example, Gen. i. 1. This was the state of things when the course of events about to be narrated commenced. Heaven and earth, the work of God, were in existence; the earth was waste—darkness was upon the deep—the Spirit of God was moving upon the waters. This *preface* being comprised in verses 1-2, the *narrative* begins in v. 3. "Thereupon (or then) God saith," etc.

Genesis xxiv. 1, 2. The first verse is a preface to the narrative which follows. 1. "Now Abraham was old and well stricken in age : and the Lord had blessed Abraham in all things." Then the narrative commences. 2. "Thereupon Abraham saith unto his eldest servant," etc.

Gen. xxxvii. 2. The former part of the verse is a preface, the narrative beginning with the last clause : "Then Joseph bringeth unto his father."

22. And this practice of introducing a regular narrative by a short preface is resorted to not only at the beginning of a distinct narrative, but also at the beginning of separate paragraphs in the narrative. The prefatory clause merely indicates that a certain fact once took place—then the sequence of certain other facts is stated. Taken together, a sentence thus formed is equivalent to a Latin sentence introduced by some conjunction, such as *quum*, *postquam*, or the like, or by a so-called *ablative absolute*.

EXAMPLES.

Gen. xli. 10. "Pharaoh, being wroth with his servants, *put me* in ward" (*kāṣaf—wai-yittēn*).

I. Samuel xxviii. 3. "Samuel being dead (or after Samuel was dead) Israel lamented." *Lit.* "Now Samuel was dead, thereupon all Israel laments him, and buries him in Ramah" (ū-*S.* mēθ, wai-yispĕdū). At chap. xxv. 1, where the statement of Samuel's death came in its proper place in the narrative, the usual form was employed (viz. wai-yāmōθ).

II. Sam. xix. 40. "And when *the king was come over*, the king kissed Barzillai" (wĕ-ham-melek *ʿā*var, wai-yi*ss*a*k*).

23. Then the speaker commences his narrative with the conjunction of sequence *wa* which shows only this, that the action denoted by the verb to which it was prefixed was later in time than the facts stated in the preface. Suppose a man to be relating some occurrence which he has witnessed, his first object is to put his hearer as far as possible in the position which he himself occupied at the time of the occurrence, to make his hearer see and hear what he himself saw and heard, and in the same order. He does not gather the facts he has to tell into artificial groups, but recounts them one by one, each in its place as it occurred. He connects them by a conjunction, which indicates that each act or event expressed by the verb to which that conjunction is prefixed is in order of time later than the act or event expressed by the verb to which the like conjunction is prefixed in the clause immediately before it. The very words of each speaker are repeated. His thoughts also are given as words—as what "he said in his heart." Thus the story flows on. No reference is

made to time, except so far as the particle *wa* indicates sequence. Each incident of the narrative, each agent or speaker that takes part in it, is brought before the hearer in due order, just as if a roll containing a series of pictures representing them in their proper places were gradually unrolled before his eyes. Thus each incident in its turn becomes present, and moves on with the words of the narrator. The narrative sets forth a series of present acts, and is not complicated by any reference to the later time at which the story is related, or to times which were future to the persons mentioned in the course of the narrative.

This habit of mind being common to both narrator and hearer, the simple forms of the Hebrew verbs supply all that is needed.

24. This original form fitly corresponded to the oral narratives of contemporary events, with which earlier and simpler races would have chiefly to do. Afterwards it came to be used as a mode of writing history : for it was a clear, lively, and intelligible mode of conveying the story of the past as well as of the present. It continued to be the only form of narration through the period in which the books were written, from which our examples are taken.

Our own habits of speech do not allow us to follow the Hebrew usage in our versions ; but, in order to understand the construction of the language, it is needful to bear this usage in mind.

CHAPTER III.

GRAMMATICAL NOTES.

The object of these notes is to show how the general rules laid down in the preceding chapter are to be applied to the clearing up of grammatical difficulties in the Hebrew text. It is not intended to point out every passage to which the rules are applicable; but rather to select certain instances whereby the meaning and extent of the rules may be made clear, and the learner may be enabled to apply them for himself to other passages.

GENESIS—CHAPTER I.

vv. 14, 15. "*Let there be lights in the firmament, and let them be for signs*" (yehī—wĕ-hāyū). Here the latter clauses of a command are expressed by Perfects *subjoined* to an Imperfect.

v. 31. eθ-kol—ăser āsāh: i.e., "*Everything of which he was the maker—every created thing.*" The words refer to the relation between the maker and the things made, not to time.

CHAPTER II.

v. 10. yippārēd — wĕ-hāyāh. "The stream at that point is divided, and in dividing becomes," etc.; the division of the one stream and the formation of the four rivers being different stages of one natural operation.

Chapter IV.

v. 1. wĕ-hā-ādām yāda₍. These words are intended as an introduction or preface to a new narrative, which begins with *wat-takar*, and is carried on from stage to stage by the use of the same particle *wa*.

v. 14. hāyīθī and hāyūh are *subjoined* Perfects which indicate further stages in the process of departing from the presence of God.

Chapter V., verses 3–6.

Here we read that :—

v. 3. " Adam lived 130 years *and* begat Seth : "

v. 4. " *And* the days of Adam after he begat Seth were 800 years, *and* he begat sons and daughters : "

v. 5. " *And* all the days that Adam lived were 930, and he died."

v. 6. " *And Seth* lived 105 years *and* begat Enos : "

Throughout these verses the word *and* represents the Hebrew ' wa,' which appears at first sight to indicate that all the facts narrated are represented as following one another in the order in which they are written. The birth of Enos would therefore appear to have taken place after the death of Adam. Yet this is contradicted by the narrative itself. Are we then to abandon the theory of the Vau of Sequence? By no means. The solution of the difficulty is this—that in pedigrees of this form there is a twofold sequence. One is a continuous lineal sequence from father to son, tracing the descent from eldest son to eldest son : the persons being all named. To set forth this sequence is the special purpose of the narrator. Besides this, there is a collateral sequence of events following the birth of the eldest son of each patriarch; the narrator taking care to mention in each case that besides the descendant named there were other descendants unnamed, and to state also the age of the patriarch at the time of his death. The former sequence is carried on through the verses 3, 6, 9, 12, 15, and so on; the latter, in the verses intervening between each couple of those numbers.

We should probably have separated these and have placed first the direct pedigree, and the other matters subsequently.

But the mode here used did not fail of being understood. Accordingly, in the Hebrew manuscripts, and in the printed text, the narrative is broken up into groups in such manner as that each group begins with the birth of the firstborn son of each patriarch, and ends with the death of that patriarch. A space is then left in the manuscript, and a symbol introduced to indicate that the sequence indicated by the first word of the next group is not an immediate sequence upon the clause preceding. This device of the Hebrew scribes is imitated by the paragraphs in our English Bible.

CHAPTER VI.

v. 21. āsaftā. This Perfect, being *subjoined* to an Imperative, becomes an Imperative. So again in the third clause, wĕ-hāyāh. "*And thou—take to thee of all food which is eaten, and gather it to thee—and be it to thee and to them for food.*"

CHAPTER VIII.

v. 17. hōṣĕ—wĕ-sārĕṣū—ū-farū—wĕ-rāvū. "*Bring forth —and let them breed—and be fruitful and multiply.*"

CHAPTER IX.

v. 16. wĕ-hāyĕθāh—ū-rĕīθī. "*So soon as the bow is in the cloud, I look upon it to remember.*"

v. 26. w-īhī. "*And let Canaan be his servant.*"

v. 27. yaft-Elōhīm. "*May God enlarge — and may he dwell—and let Canaan be his servant.*"

CHAPTER X.

v. 8. wĕ-Kūs yālad eθ Nimrōd. In this verse all that is asserted is the fact that Kush was father of Nimrod. There is no attempt to define the precise place of Nimrod in the historic series. So throughout this chapter.

CHAPTER XI.

v. 9. ʿal-kēn kārū. "*Therefore doth one call.*" The Perfect here indicates a custom.

vv. 10-26. Here we have a pedigree extending from Shem to Abram. It differs throughout from that in chap. v. in this respect, that there is no statement of the whole length of life or of the death of each patriarch. In the earlier part it differs also in another respect. In v. 12 and again in v. 14 the difficulty which was noticed in the notes on chap. v. arising from the use of the *wa* throughout, is avoided by a change of structure. The *wa* is dropped and the sequence manifestly broken, so as to leave no apparent contradiction.. It is singular that in all the later parts of the narrative this device is not resorted to, but the form which has been considered above (chap. v. 3-6) is retained. Here, as before, the Hebrew editors of the text have, by spaces and symbols, marked the places where the sequence is not immediate.

CHAPTER XII.

v. 1. wai-yōmer. " *Then saith the Lord.*"
Here again the difficulty of a double sequence presents itself. The direct sequence belongs to the life of Abram ; which is the primary subject of the narrative. The sequence in the last verse of chap. xi. is a divergent or secondary one. In chap. xii. 1, the direct sequence is resumed.

v. 2. "*And become a blessing*" (hĕyēh).

v. 12. kī yiru—wĕ-āmĕrū—wĕ-hārĕgū-ōθī—wĕ-ōθāk yĕχaiyu. "*In case they see, then they will say—and will kill me, but thee they will save alive.*" After the word *me* (ōθī) the structure is varied : the dependence is severed, and the concluding clause takes the form of a direct and independent assertion ; though, for the purpose of emphasis and contrast, the pronoun 'thee' (ōθāk) is transferred to the commencement of the clause.

v. 13. The Perfect χayĕθāh is *subjoined* to the Imperfect yītāv.

CHAPTER XIII.

vv. 5, 6. These two verses are a *preface*, introduced to

indicate the state of things at the time when the strife about to be indicated arose.

vv. 11, 12. wai-yippārĕdū—yāsav—wĕ-yāsav. The Perfects are used not to express any new fact, but simply to explain the word yippārĕdū.

CHAPTER XIV.

v. 16. The Perfect hĕshīv follows the time of yūsev, no other time being indicated.

CHAPTER XV.

v. 6. wĕ-heĕmin. *"And at the time last mentioned, whilst he was hearing the words spoken, he believed."*

CHAPTER XVII.

vv. 5–8. The Imperfect yikkārē belongs to a future time, as shown by the word ⸰ōd. To this Imperfect are *subjoined*, in v. 6, hifrēθī—nĕθattī; in v. 7, hăkīmōθī; in v. 8, nĕθattī; and finally, hāyīθī. All these Perfects mark successive stages in the transaction or history. The last clause of v. 6, *"even kings out of thee shall come,"* is an independent clause, by way of parenthesis.

v. 19. wĕ-kārāθā. *"And thou shalt call."* The time of calling being already fixed in the reference to a son yet to be born.

CHAPTER XVIII.

v. 19. lĕ-ma⸰an hāvī. *"To the end that the Lord may be the bringer of all,"* etc. The Perfect here expresses not any specific act, but a permanent relation.

v. 25. wĕ-hāyāh. "*So that the state of things be this:* *as the righteous, so the wicked.*"

CHAPTER XIX.

v. 3. wai yaⲁaś misteh—u-maṣṣoθ āfāh—misteh refers only to that which was to be drunk, and not to that which was to be eaten; therefore, to mark the two distinct operations, the wĕ of the latter clause is not prefixed to the verb, but to the noun.

CHAPTER XX.

v. 6. wā-eχśōk. "*And so* (thereupon) *I withheld thee.*"
v. 7. wĕ-χĕyeh. "*And* (so doing) *live.*"

CHAPTER XXI.

vv. 24, 25. wai-yōmer A.—wĕ-hokīaχ A. "Then Abraham said—and Abraham reproved." The reproof was not part of a prior or other transaction, but of the same transaction of which the narration commences in v. 22. Abraham takes the oath required of him against wrongful dealing on his part, and goes on to complain of wrongful dealing on the part of Abimelech. The words of the oath are given expressly, "I swear"; of the reproof, the substance only is given. Both the oath and the reproof were comprised in one unbroken discourse. This is indicated by the use of the *subjoined* Perfect.

CHAPTER XXIII.

v. 4. eⲕborāh. "*Let me bury.*"
vv. 11–13. In v. 11, by the word nāθattī Ephron expresses, not a single act, but the relation which he bears to the other party in the transaction: "The field I *give*

—I am *a giver.*" In like manner, in v. 13, Abraham describes his part by the form nāθattī kesef. "I *am a giver of silver.* I purchase for money. I do not take it on any other terms."

Chapter XXIV.

v. 14. wĕ-hāyāh. This Perfect is *subjoined* to the Imperative haḵreh-nā in v. 12, and takes thence a precative sense.

v. 29. Here the sequence is broken; and a fact already existing is stated, as an introduction to the following narrative.

Chapter XXV.

v. 5. The narrative interrupted at v. 3 is here resumed. The vv. 3-4 are a parenthesis, giving some further information as to the family of Keturah.

Chapter XXVI.

v. 3. wĕ-ehyeh. "*I will be with thee.*" A promise following a command. In vv. 3-4 the first stage in the train of promised blessing is expressed by the Imperfect ettēn; the latter stages, by the *subjoined* Perfects χakīmōθī—hirbēθī—nāθattī—hiθbārĕkū.

v. 5. wai-yismōr. "*Not only heard my commandments, but went on to keep them.*"

Chapter XXVII.

v. 6. The sequence is here broken, to show that the discourse of the mother to her favourite son began before Esau had gone forth.

v. 15. "anōkī ⸱immāk ū-sĕmartī.   "*I (will be) with thee and keep thee.*"

CHAPTER XXIX.

v. 2. ya*sk*u.   This form is here used to express an act performed from time to time.   The context shows it to be past.

v. 3. wĕ-neesfū — wĕ-gālĕlū — wĕ-his*k*ū — wĕ-hēsīvū. Concurrent Perfects. "*Whenever the flocks were gathered, then they rolled away the stone, and watered the sheep and put the stone again in his place.*"

v. 26. *Lit.* "*It is not done so in our place, to give the younger before the elder.*"

vv. 16, 17. These two verses are a preface or introduction to the narrative which commences in v. 18.

CHAPTER XXX.

v. 25. "*Send me away, and let me go*" (elkāh).

v. 27. ni𝜒astī wa-ivārak-ēnī.   "I was *an observer, then* (after that time) *the Lord blessed me* for thy sake"; *i.e.,* "from the time at which I began to observe, the Lord hath been blessing me for thy sake."

CHAPTER XXXIII.

v. 13. ū-dĕfākū-m —ʾwā-me𝜃ū.   Concurrent Perfects. "*When they overdrive—then they die*"; *i.e.,* overdriving will be their death.

CHAPTER XXXV.

v. 3. hā-⸱ōneh ō𝜃ī—wa-yĕhī ⸱immādī.   *Lit.* "*Who answered me, and then became with me (i.e., thenceforward became my companion and guide) in the journey."* Compare chap. xxviii. 20.

Chapter XXXVII.

v. 19. bū. *"Is come."*

v. 15. hărīmōθĭ ḳōl-ĭ—wū-ekrā. First came a scream or loud cry, then an articulate call for help. wū for wa before Alef.

Chapter XL.

vv. 13–14. " Thou wilt return to thy former office ; not that only, but thou wilt moreover remember me." The form *kĭ-im* appears to add something positive to a preceding negative statement, or something specific to a preceding general statement.

v. 22. wĕ-lō zūkar — wai-yiskaχ-ēhu. *i.e.,* The chief butler did not at the time of his restoration to his office remember Joseph, and after a time he forgat him altogether.

Chapter XLI.

v. 30. ăχarē-hen. These words give a future time to ḳāmū. *"After the seven years of plenty, there shall arise seven years of famine."*

Chapter XLIII.

v. 14. wĕ-El-Shaddai—yitten. A pause is to be made after the Divine name : *" God Almighty—may He give."* A similar instance occurs in verse 29.

Chapter XLIV.

v. wa-ʿχappēś—hēχēl—killāh. The Perfects indicate, not a new act, but the mode in which the act expressed by the Imperfect was performed.

v. 33. wĕ-han-na‹ar ya‹al. "*And the lad*—let *him go up.*"

Chapter XLV.

v. 10. "*Come down hither—and dwell.*" The Perfect yūsavtā is subjoined to the Imperative rĕdāh in verse 9.

v. 13. "*And tell.*" This Perfect higgadtem follows ămartem in verse 9; and, like that, is subjoined to ‹ālū in the same verse.

Verse 12 is a parenthesis.

Chapter XLVII.

v. 30. wĕ-sākavtī—u-nĕsāθa-nī. "*But let me lie with my fathers, and do thou carry me out of Egypt.*" These Perfects are subjoined to the Precative in the preceding verse.

Chapter XLVIII.

vv. 15, 16. "*God*—the *God which hath fed me—may He bless the lads.*"

v. 21. "*I die, and (when I die) then shall come to pass this state of things*—namely, *God shall be with you, and bring you again unto the land of your fathers.*"

Exodus—Chapter III.

v. 10. "*I send thee unto Pharaoh, and bring thou forth my people.*"

v. 18. wĕ-nizbĕχāh. "*And let us sacrifice.*"

v. 20. wĕ-salaχtī. "*Then (when the king refuses to let you go) will I stretch out my hand.*"

CHAPTER IV.

v. 8. wĕ-hāyāh. This verb takes a future time from the words, "*if they will not believe.*"

v. 14. wĕ-rāa-kā — wĕ-śamaχ. "*And when he seeth thee, he will be glad.*"   Concurrent Perfects.

vv. 21-23. "*When thou goest to return into Egypt, see, all the wonders which I have put into thy hand, then* (when thou art come into Egypt) *shalt thou do them before Pharaoh. Thou shalt say, Thus saith* (koh āmar) *the Lord* (this is the message, or purpose, of the Lord), *Israel is my son. So* (in consequence of this being so) *I say to thee, Let my son go; thereupon thou refusest, behold, I slay thy son.*" At the time when the punishment, announced in the concluding words, takes effect, the command and the refusal to obey will be already past. Accordingly, they are stated in the ordinary form of a narrative of past events.

CHAPTER VI.

vv. 3-5. wā-ērā. The verb expresses simply the fact of appearing. The mention of Abraham, Isaac, and Jacob suggests past time, and indicates that the appearance was repeated from time to time.

CHAPTER XII.

v. 4. wĕ-lākaχ. "*And if the house be too little, then shall he and his neighbours take.*"

v. 13. wĕ-rāīθī — wĕ-pāsaχtī. "*When (so soon as) I see—then I will pass over.*"

v. 22. ū-lĕkaχtem. This Perfect and the others which follow in this verse are subjoined to the Imperative saχătū in v. 21. " *Do this now, and further observe it as an ordinance for ever.*"

v. 23. wĕ- āvar. " *Then (when the directions just given are carried out) will the Lord pass through.*"

v. 24. " ū-sĕmartem. " *And observe.*" This is the last in the train of Perfects subjoined to the Imperative saχătū.

v. 27. " *Then ye (shall) say.*"

Chapter XIII.

v. 5. " *Then thou shalt keep this service.*"

Chapter XVII.

v. 9. Here nīṣṣāv expresses, not a single act, but a state —not merely standing on the hill-top, but occupying a post there for an indefinite time, even so long as the battle might last.

v. 11. wĕ-hāyāh ka-ăser yārīm—wĕ-gāvar. Lit. "*And there becometh this state of things; whenever Moses lifts up his hands—then Israel prevails.*"

Chapter XVIII.

v. 8. wai-yaṣṣil-ēm. "*All the trouble which came upon them, and then (after all) the Lord delivered them.*"

vv. 19-20. wĕ-hēvēθā — wĕ-hizhartā — wĕ-hōda·tā. All these Perfects are subjoined to the Imperative hĕyēh. "*Be (become) thou—and bring—and teach—and shew.*"

vv. 21-22. wĕ-śamtā—wĕ-sāfĕtū. These Perfects are subjoined to the Imperfect θeχĕzeh. "*Moreover thou shalt provide—and shalt place—and they shall judge.*"

Chapter XXV.

v. 2. The whole passage from mē-ēθ kol-īš to the end of v. 7, is a parenthesis.

v. 8. wĕ-ʿāśū l-ī mikdaš wē-šākantī. The Perfect ʿāśū is subjoined to the Imperative yikχū in v. 2. "*And let them make me a sanctuary. Then will I dwell among them.*"

v. 15. This verse is a parenthesis.

v. 22. wĕ-nōʿadtī. "*Then (these things being done) will I meet thee there.*"

Chapter XXVIII.

wē-ʿāsīθā. This Perfect is subjoined to the Imperative hakrēv in v. 1. "*And make thou.*"

v. 42. "*And make.*"

v. 43. wē-lō yiśū ʿāwōn wā-mēθū. "*And thereby they shall not bear iniquity, and (in bearing it) die.*"

Chapter XXIX.

v. 3. This Perfect nāθattā is subjoined to the Imperative lĕkaχ in v. 1.

v. 12. These words wĕ-eθ-kol mizbēaχ are a parenthesis; the *wĕ* being prefixed, not to the verb, but to a noun; and the original Imperfect form being resumed.

v. 14. This verse also is a parenthesis, following the same construction.

Chapter XXX.

v. 1. wĕ-ʿāṣīθā. "*And thou shalt make:*" thus resuming the construction which was interrupted at v. 35 of the last chapter.

v. 33. Lit. "A *man who shall compound*" etc., which is equivalent to "*If any man shall compound*" etc. So that wĕ-nikraθ becomes a regular statement of the result to follow on that supposition, "*Then shall he be cut off.*"

CHAPTER XXXII.

v. 8. Lit. "*They made—then they bowed down to it— then they sacrificed to it.*" The *wa* is used to mark the stages of their apostasy.

v. 23. "*So they said unto me.*"

CHAPTER XXXIII.

vv. 7-11. From wĕ-hāyāh in the middle of v. 7 to the end of v. 11 we have no longer a narrative of specific facts happening at certain times, but a statement of the ordinary and customary course of things which arose as soon as Moses removed the tabernacle to a place outside of the camp. The *wā* and its Imperfects are dropped, and instead we find *we* with Perfects indicating the several stages in the new order of things. "*And it became the custom — every man that seeketh the Lord, goeth out—.*" "*Also it became the custom—when Moses goeth out, straight-way rise up all the people and take their stand—and look—.*" "*Also it became the custom, when Moses goeth into the tabernacle straightway descendeth — and standeth — and He speaketh,*" etc.

v. 10. wĕ-rāāh—wĕ-kām. Concurrent Perfects. "*And whenever the people saw—then they rose up.*"

v. 11. wĕ-dibber. The writer repeats the closing words

of v. 9, and goes on to explain the manner of the speaking there mentioned.

Chapter XXXIV.

v. 33. Lit. "*Then Moses ceases speaking with them, then (after ceasing to speak) he puts on his face a veil.*"

Chapter XXXVI.

E. V. "*Then wrought Bezaleel and Aholiab.*" If this had been the meaning, it must have been expressed in Hebrew by *wā* with the Imperfect. The form wĕ-hāyāh indicates a grammatical dependence of this verse on the last verse of the chapter preceding. "*In order that Bezaleel and Aholiab may work (be the regular workers).*" The beginning of the work is narrated in the following verses.

Chapter XL.

v. 29. Here the sequence is broken, in order to introduce a mention of facts which were going on concurrently with some of the facts just narrated. Whilst one set of men were, by direction of Moses, setting up the tabernacle and putting in their places the ark, the table of shew bread, and other things appertaining to the tabernacle; another set, also under his direction, were putting the brazen altar and the laver in their places outside of the tabernacle.

v. 31. "*Moses and Aaron washed their hands and feet thereat,*" *i.e.* they did so regularly and habitually, as is expressly stated in the next verse. The Perfect is used to indicate the custom.

LEVITICUS—CHAPTER IV.

v. 3. wĕ-ha*k*rīv. " *Then shall he offer.*"

vv. 11, 12. wĕ-hōṣī. In the beginning of v. 12, continues the regular series of subjoined Perfects. But v. 11 disturbs the construction. It is, however, an irregularity which does not affect the questions with which alone we are here concerned, viz. the use and meaning of the Forms called *Perfect* and *Imperfect*. The same irregularity appears in the LXX.

CHAPTER XIV.

v. 48. wĕ-im bō yāvō—wĕ-*t*ihar. "If the priest shall, by actual entrance into the house and by personal inspection, have satisfied himself that the plague hath not spread in the house, *then* he shall pronounce it clean."

CHAPTER XVII.

v. 10. Whatsoever man, etc. i.e. " *If any man shall eat, then (whensoever he shall eat) will I set my face against him.*" A similar construction occurs below in v. 13 and again in xxiv. 15.

CHAPTER XIX.

v. 12. lō-θissāvĕʿū — we-χillalta. " *Ye shall not swear by my name falsely, and· thereby profane the name of thy God.*"

v. 29. " *Lest the land fall to whoredom and the land be full of wickedness.*" The subjoined Perfect marks a later stage in the course of evil ; namely, the general demoralization of which a prevalence of unchastity would be the beginning.

Chapter XXV.

v. 36. al-tiκκaχ—wĕ-yārc̄θū—wĕ-χāi. "*Take not usury of him, but fear thy God, and let thy brother live.*"

Chapter XXVI.

vv. 40-42. wĕ-hiθwaddū — wĕ-zākartī. Concurrent Perfects. "*Whensoever they confess their iniquity, then will I remember my covenant.*"

Numbers—Chapter I.

v. 48. "*Then spake the Lord.*"

v. 50. we-attah hafκēd. "*But do thou appoint.*"

Chapter III.

v. 4. ū-vānīm lō-hāyū lā-hem. "*And they had no children.*" The Perfect is here used to state circumstances existing at the time of the fact last mentioned, and accompanying that fact. It is equivalent to saying "*and they died without issue.*"

v. 44. wĕ-hāyū. "*And let them be mine.*" This Perfect is subjoined to κaχ in the beginning of the verse.

Chapter IV.

v. 15. lā-yiggĕū—wā-mc̄θū. One transaction, "*They shall not touch—and in touching die.*"

Chapter V.

v. 22. ū-vāū. These words continue the imprecation, "*And may this water go.*"

Chapter VIII.

v. 18. wā-eκκaχ. "*So I took the Levites instead of all the first-born—then I gave the Levites to Aaron.*"

v. 22. bāū. "*And after that went the Levites (regularly and habitually) in, to do their service in the tabernacle.*"

CHAPTER IX.

v. 21. wĕ-naȧlāh — wĕ-nāsāȧū. "*Whenever (the cloud) was taken up, then they journeyed.*" A like construction recurs in x. 17.

CHAPTER X.

v. 14. From this verse forward up to v. 27, the Imperfect with *wa* is not used. The statement comprised in these verses relates, not to any specific facts, but to the custom and fixed order according to which the march of the tribes was conducted, so as to maintain unaltered the relative positions of the several portions of the host. The Perfect therefore is employed throughout. At the close of v. 28 the writer resumes his narrative of the facts of the journey. "*So they set forward. Then said Moses to Hobad.*"

CHAPTER XI.

v. 25. wa-yiθnabbĕū—wĕ-lō yāśāfū. "*Then they acted as prophets, and did not add,*" i.e. they did not act as prophets after that time. So that this Perfect does not indicate a new fact or event in the narrative, but merely the nature of the fact last mentioned, viz. that the gift was temporary.

v. 31. āmĕrū. Whilst Caleb was encouraging the people to go up, his companions were advising them to the contrary. The Perfect refers to the time given in the verse preceding.

Chapter XIV.

v. 15. wĕ-hēmattā̄—wĕ-āmĕrū. "*When Thou killest (as Thou threatenest to do) all this people, then will the nations speak.*"

Chapter XIX.

v. 3. ū-nĕθattem. "*Then (that being done) shall ye give.*"

vv. 11-16. These verses, which state the circumstances under which a person will become unclean, are introduced by way of parenthesis in the midst of the directions given for the removal of uncleanness. The regular construction is resumed, and the directions are completed, in vv. 17-19.

Chapter XX.

vv. 14, 15. hat-tĕlāāh—wai-yērĕdū. "*The trouble that befell us. Then (after that) our fathers went down to Egypt.*" The trouble then was the famine.

v. 24. yēāsēf Ahă̄rōn. "*Let Aaron be gathered to his people.*"

Chapter XXI.

v. 34. al-tīrā̄—we-āsīθā. "*Fear not, but do.*" The intervening words being a parenthesis.

Chapter XXII.

v. 41. wai-yar—mis-som. "*And shewed to* him from thence."

Chapter XXXI.

v. 8. wĕ-eθ-malkē Midyān hārĕgū. "*And even the kings they slew.*" The Perfect here states no new fact, but serves to make more clear and decided the general statement preceding, namely, that all the males were slain.

v. 50. wan-nakrēv. *"And so we bring,"* i.e. having counted the men of war under our command and found not one missing, we in consequence thereof bring an offering.

CHAPTER XXXII.

v. 15. kī yesūvun — wĕ-yāsaf — wĕ-siχattem. Lit. *" In case ye turn back, then He will yet again leave them. Then, if He so leave them, ye will be the destroyers of this people."*

vv. 34-37. wai-yivnū—ū-vĕnē R. bānū. *" Then (after Moses had assigned the land) the children of Gad built the places named in vv. 34-36: and, during the same time, the children of Reuben built the places named in vv. 37-8."*

DEUTERONOMY—CHAPTER II.

v. 12. *"Also in Seir dwelt the Horim beforetime; but the children of Esau dispossessed them, and after a time destroyed them. So they dwelt there in their stead."*

CHAPTER III.

v. 2. See note on Numbers xxi. 34.

CHAPTER IV.

v. 6. ū-sĕmartem. This Perfect is subjoined to the Imperative rĕēh in v. 5.

v. 15. we-nismartem. This Perfect is subjoined to the Imperative hissāmer in v. 9.

v. 29. ū-viκkastem—ū-māṣūθā. *"When ye seek, then shalt thou find."*

v. 33. wai-yĕχī. *"And after that continue to live."*

v. 39. wĕ-yūdaˌtā. *" Know therefore."* This Perfect is

subjoined to hissămĕrū in v. 23; all the verses from 25 to 38 inclusive being a parenthesis.

v. 42. wĕ-nās — wā-χūi. *"When he fleeth unto one of these cities, then he liveth."*

CHAPTER V.

v. 29 (E. V. 32). ū-sĕmartem la-ᴕásōθ. *" Observe therefore to do."* At this point the construction which was interrupted at v. 41 of chap. iv. is resumed; two long parentheses filling up the interval, viz. chap. iv. 41-49, and chap. v. 1-28 (E. V. 1—31).

CHAPTER VI.

v. 3. wĕ-sāmaᴕtā—wĕ-samartā—la-ᴕásōθ. *"When thou hearest, then shalt thou observe to do it."*

v. 5. wĕ-āhavtā. *"And love thou."* This Perfect is subjoined to the Imperative sĕmaᴕ in v. 4.

v. 6. wĕ-hāyū. *"And let these words be;"* thus continuing the construction of the preceding verse. So likewise in vv. 7-10. *"And teach thou—and talk—and bind—and let them be—and write—and let it be."*

CHAPTER VII.

v. 1. wĕ-nāsal. *"And cast out."* This Perfect is subjoined to the Imperfect yĕvīă-kā.

v. 9. wĕ-yādaᴕtā. *"And thou shalt know."* This verse continues the construction of vv. 1-5, the vv. 6-8 being a parenthesis.

CHAPTER VIII.

v. 18. wĕ-zākartā. *" But remember."* This Perfect is

subjoined to hissamer in v. 11, the vv. 12-17 being a parenthesis.

CHAPTER X.

v. 16. ū-maltem. "*Circumcise therefore.*" In the foregoing verses nothing appears to account for the use of this form, unless it be allowable to treat the whole passage from chap. ix. 8 to chap. x. 15 as a long parenthesis; or rather, as two parentheses, of which the second begins at chap. x. 12. This inference, grounded on grammatical considerations only, is strengthened by the connexion of thought between chap. ix. v. 7, and this verse.

CHAPTER XI.

v. 1. wĕ-āhavtā. "*Therefore thou shalt love.*" This Perfect is subjoined to the Imperfects in v. 20 of the last chapter.

v. 2. w-īdaʿtem. "*And ye shall know (for I speak not with your children, which have not known, and have not seen) the chastisement.*

v. 14. wĕ-nāθattī—wĕ-āsaftū. "*Then will I give—and thou shalt gather in.*"

CHAPTER XII.

v. 30. ēkāh yaʿavdū. "*How did these nations serve their gods?*" The Imperfect is used to express an act repeated from time to time. *What forms of sacrifice and prayer did these nations use at their regular times of worship?*

v. 31. ʿāśū. "*They do habitually.*" yiśrĕfū. "*They burn from time to time.*"

Chapter XIII.

v. 5 (E. V. v. 6). ū-viɑrtā. This Perfect is subjoined to yūmāθ in the earlier part of the verse. "*By the death of the false prophet shall the evil be put away.*"

Chapter XV.

v. 6. kī-Y. bērak-ka—wĕ-haɑ̆vattā. "*In case the Lord shall have blessed thee—then shalt thou lend.*" The whole context, from chap. xii. 1 downward, shows that a future time is here contemplated.

Chapter XVII.

vv. 2-3. ɑ̆ser yaɑašeh—wai-yēlek wai-yaɑ̆vŏd—wai-yistaχū. Here the grammatical form, ordinarily used for the purpose of narrating facts actually past, is employed for the purpose of stating a case supposed to have happened, and to have been ascertained to be matter of fact, before the time at which the command now given is to take effect.

v. 12. wĕ-hā-īs ɑ̆ser yaɑ̆šeh—wa-mēθ ū-viɑrtā. "*And the man* (i.e. *if any man*) *shall do—then shall he die, and thereby shalt thou put away the evil.*"

Chapter XX.

v. 18. yĕlammĕdū — wa-χɑ̆t̄aθem. "*To the end that they may not teach you and you* (*being so taught*) *sin.*" These words express one operation, the cause and its effects.

Chapter XXVI.

v. 16. wĕ-sāmartā wĕ-ɑāśiθā. "*Thou shalt therefore keep and do them,*" etc. The relation between the people of Israel and their God carries with it an obligation on their part to render immediate obedience to every command which proceeds from Him.

Chapter XXVIII.

The blessings in vv. 3-6 of this chapter and the curses in vv. 16-19 are in the E. V. rendered as promises of good and as threats of evil. Yet they are expressed in words which, in form and position, closely resemble those which are used in chap. xxvii. vv. 15-26, and should therefore be rendered in the same manner. In accordance with this view, the verses immediately following in each case are in the precative or imprecative form. Thus vv. 7, 8, 9, *"May the Lord cause"* etc. *May the Lord command* etc. *May the Lord establish* etc.

v. 12. yiftaχ Y. *"May the Lord open"* etc. wĕhilwīθā. *"Then (if he so open, etc.) shalt thou lend."*

v. 14. *"And if thou go not aside."*

v. 20. yesallaχ Y. bĕ-kā. *"The Lord send upon thee."* A like form recurs in vv. 21, 22, 24, 25, 27, 28.

v. 35. yakkĕ-kāh. *"The Lord smite thee."*

v. 36. yōlēk. *"The Lord bring thee, etc.—then (when thou art brought thither) shalt thou serve."*

v. 49. yiśśā Y. *"The Lord bring."*

Chapter XXIX.

v. 8 (E. V. v. 9). ū-sĕmartem. This Perfect is subjoined to the Imperfect θēdĕ⸲ū in v. 5. The intervening vv. 6-7 being a parenthesis. *"To the end that ye may know that*

I am the Lord—and that ye may keep the words of this covenant."

Chapter XXXIII.

vv. 27-8. wa-igāres—wai-yōmer—wai-yiskōn. *" There-fore he thrust out the enemy—and said, Destroy them. So Israel dwelt in safety alone."*

Joshua—Chapter II.

v. 6. wĕ-hī heἐlāθ-ām. A breach of sequence: the act of hiding having preceded the act of answering the king.

v. 22. wa-ivaksū. *" Then they search."* This does not mean that the pursuers start afresh on their pursuit after the last fact mentioned; but that the pursuers continue their search after the last fact introduced by a *wa*, viz. the fact of the spies taking up their abode in the mountain.

Chapter IV.

v. 16. "Command the priests—that they come up out of Jordan " (wĕ-yaἀlū). Here the dependent Imperfect expresses the *purport* of the command.

Chapter VI.

vv. 5 - 6. kī-yēṣĕū — wĕ-nasnū — wĕ-yāṣĕū. *" In case they come out against us—then we will flee before them and they will come out after us, even until we have drawn them away from the city."* The Perfect yāṣĕū is contemporaneous with the Perfect nasnū.

The concluding words of v. 6, which disturb the con-

struction, are not found in the LXX. It is apparently an
error of transcription, a repetition of the last words of
v. 5, owing to the recurrence of the words bā-risōnāh.

Chapter VIII.

vv. 18-19. The men in ambush had arisen and were
already standing up—and, when Joshua stretched out his
hands, then they began to run towards the city. This
is shown by the breach of sequence at the commencement
of v. 19. wĕ-hā-ōrēv *k*ām.

Chapter IX.

v. 21. wai-yōmĕrū. Lit. " *Then say the princes*—Let
them live. *So they become hewers of wood* " (wai-yihyū).

Chapter X.

v. 1. Here in an indirect narrative we find *wa* with the
Imperfect used in exactly the same way as in a direct
narrative : wai-yaχarīmāh, i.e. " *Not only taken Ai, but
gone further and utterly destroyed it.*"

Chapter XIX.

vv. 49-50. waī-yittēnū—nāθĕnū. " *Then the children of
Israel gave an inheritance to Joshua—they gave him the city
which he asked.*" The Perfect is here used in the latter
clause, because it does not carry the narrative forward, but
only explains a transaction formerly mentioned, and refers
to the time of that transaction.

Chapter XX.

vv. 2-3. "*Appoint—that they may be.*"
v. 4. wē-nās—wĕ-ḏamad—wĕ-dibbēr—wĕ-āsĕfū. "*When*

one hath fled—and hath stood—and declared, then shall they take him in."

CHAPTER XXII.

v. 1. sĕmartem — wat-tismĕ⸱ū. "*Ye kept all that Moses commanded you. And, since that time, ye obey my voice.*"

v. 17. wa-ihī han-negef. "*A grievous iniquity, the consequence whereof was the plague.*"

v. 18. wĕ-attem. "And, notwithstanding that, ye are turning away this day from following the Lord ; *and this is the state of things*—ye are rebelling this day against the Lord, and to-morrow with the whole congregation will He be wroth " (wĕ-hāyāh).

v. 25. wĕ-hisbīθū. This Perfect is subjoined to yōmĕrū in v. 24.

v. 28. wĕ-hāyāh kī-yōmĕrū—wĕ-āmarnū. Concurrent Perfects. "*When it cometh to pass (becometh the state of things) that they say—then say we.*"

CHAPTER XXIII.

vv. 4-8. These verses are to be regarded as a parenthesis. In this parenthesis the Perfect χăzaktem is subjoined to the Imperative rĕū in v. 4.

CHAPTER XXIV.

v. 7. wat-tirenāh. "*Then your eyes saw.*"

JUDGES—CHAPTER I.

v. 8. "Then the children of Judah fought against Jerusalem, and they took it—and they smote it (*i.e.* the

people), and the city *they set on fire* " (sillĕχū bā-ēs).
The Perfect is here used to express an event contemporaneous with the event last mentioned; the city being
set on fire, whilst the slaughter was going on.

Chapter II.

v. 1. aꞁleh. Here the narrative commences without
any *Preface* or introductory clause. Therefore the Imperfect alone is employed without the *wa :* there being
nothing for the *wa* to refer back to. The past time is
clearly indicated by the reference to Egypt.

v. 3. wĕ-gam-āmartī. *" Wherefore also I say, I will
not."* The Preterite here indicates a word (or *purpose*)
belonging to the present time, no other time being indicated.

Chapter III.

v. 23. wai-yisgōr—wĕ-nāꞁal. The Perfect nāꞁal is subjoined to the Imperfect yisgōr, because the acts indicated
by the two verbs are parts of one transaction.

v. 24. wĕ-hū yāṣā—wĕ-ăꞁvādā-w bāū. Concurrent
Perfects. *" So soon as he* (Ehud) *went forth, his* (Eglon's)
servants came."

Chapter IV.

v. 1. wĕ Ehūd mēθ. Lit. *"And Ehud was dead,"* i.e.
was dead at the time when the people again did evil.

v. 21. *" She smote—and she fastened it into the ground,
for he was fast asleep. So he—and then he died."* The LXX.
render yāꞁaf by ἐσκοτώθη.

Chapter XI.

v. 8. lākēn — savnū — wĕ-hālaktā. "*For that very reason* (namely, our distress) *have we come back to thee; and, for that reason, wilt thou go with us and fight.*" The condition of the people of Gilead imposes a duty on Jephthah.

Chapter XII.

vv. 10-15. "Then died Ibzūn—and after him Elon *began to judge Israel,* and *he continued to judge* Israel ten years : then Elon died. Then after him Abdon *began to judge Israel;* and *he continued to judge* Israel eight years. Then Abdon died." Here yispōt is used throughout both for beginning, and for continuing, to act as judge. The context in every case shows in which of the senses the words are to be taken. Contrast this with Judges xvi. 31, where the narrator, looking back upon the whole judgeship of Samson as one fact complete and ended, uses the Perfect sāfat.

Chapter XIII.

vv. 2-3. *Lit.* "There was a certain man—whose name was Manoah, and his wife was barren and bare not. Then appeared an angel of the Lord unto the woman and said, Behold now thou wast barren and barest not, and thou dost conceive and bear a son."

These forms hinnēh-nā in v. 3, and again hinnāk in v. 5, suggest a present time. The LXX. render χārāh in v. 5 by εν γαστρὶ ἔχεις.

Chapter XVI.

v. 18. wĕ-ɑlū — wai-yaɑlū. "*And when they went*

up, then they brought." The construction of this short *Preface* is similar to that of I. Sam. vi. 16, "*And when the five Lords of the Philistines saw it, then they returned."*

Chapter XVIII.

v. 17. bāū—lākĕχū. *"As soon as they came, they took."*

Chapter XIX.

v. 4. " *Then his father-in-law detaineth him. So he abides with him three days. Then they eat and drink"* (wai-yōkĕlū). The act expressed by yōkĕlū follows in order of time on the act expressed by the last Imperfect with *wa*, namely, the word yesev (*he abides*), not on the end of the time during which the former act lasted.

Chapter XX.

v. 13. wĕ-lō avū. The Perfect here expresses the state of mind of the men of Benjamin at the time when the message just mentioned was delivered to them.

I. Samuel—Chapter I.

, v. 3. wĕ-ālāh. This Perfect expresses a custom. "*And this man went up regularly — he was one who habitually attended the festivals."*

v. 3. wai-yizbaχ E. wĕ-nāθan. " *He offers, and out of that offering gives."* The Imperfect and the Perfect indicate two stages of one transaction.

v. 15. The clause wĕ-yayin — lō-sāθīθī is a parenthesis. " I *am a woman of a sorrowful spirit—sorrow, not wine, being the cause of what you see—and so, being sorrowful, I pour out my soul in prayer"* (wū-espōk).

CHAPTER II.

v. 28. wā-ettĕnāh. *"And after that went on to give."*

CHAPTER IV.

v. 11. wa-ărōn E. nil*k*ā*χ*. A broken sequence. *"And in the course of the battle (mentioned in v. 10) the ark was taken, and the two sons of Eli were slain."*

v. 14. wĕ-hā-ī*s* mihar wai-yāvō. "Whilst the cry of the men of the city was ringing in Eli's ears, and he was greatly alarmed thereby, the man sped on through the town, and so reached Eli and told him."

CHAPTER V.

vv. 6-7. wai-yirū — wĕ-āmĕrū. Literally, *" Then the men of Ashdod see that it is so, and then and there they resolve,* The ark shall not abide with us."

CHAPTER VI.

v. 8. wĕ-ē*θ* kel*ē*i—tā*s*īmū. This is a parenthesis, interrupting the enumeration of the acts to be done. The parenthesis ends with the words miṣ-ṣidd-ō.

v. 15. wĕ-ha Lewīyim hōrīdū. "Now the Levites had taken down the ark and put it on the stone."

CHAPTER VII.

vv. 15-16. wai-yi*s*pō*t* S. — wĕ-hālak — wĕ-sāvav — wĕ-sūfa*t*. Here the continued action of Samuel as judge during a specified time is expressed by an Imperfect. Then follow Perfects, each having wĕ prefixed. These indicate no new fact or time, but only the manner in which the office was habitually discharged. *Lit.* "After

that time Samuel *continued to act* as judge all the days of
his life. And *it was his custom to travel* from year to
year, and *visit* on his circuit Bethel, etc., and *to act as
judge* at all those places."

Chapter VIII.

v. 14. "And he *will take* your fields—*and give them* to
his servants." Two stages of one transaction (yi*kka*χ wĕ-
nāθan).

Chapter IX.

v. 5. hēmmāh bāū—we S. āmar. "*As soon as they were
come—Saul said.*"

v. 6. yaggīd — ăser halaknū. "Will tell us of our
way which we have taken and are now travelling upon,
whether it be the right or the wrong way."

v. 8. wĕ-nāθattī—wĕ-higgīd. *Lit.* "When I give—
then he tells."

Chapter X.

v. 2. ū-māṣāθā. "*Then thou shalt find.*" The time of
the finding is shown to be future by the words "*When
thou art gone from me to-day.*"

v. 5. wĕ-hēmmāh miθnabbĕīm. "*And they shall be
prophesying,*" i.e. at the time when thou meetest them.

Chapter XII.

v. 17. Lit. "*So know ye and see.*"

Chapter XIV.

v. 24. wai-yōel. "*Then* Samuel adjured the people."

v. 52. wĕ-rāāh — wai-yaasfēhū. "*And during the time*

just mentioned—i.e. the continuance of the war—*when Saul saw any strong man, he thereupon took him.*"

Chapter XV.

v. 30. "*And return with me. If thou do so, then shall I worship the Lord thy God.*"

v. 34. wai-yĕlek Se. — we Saūl ,ālāh. Here the Perfect is used in the latter clause, because the journey therein mentioned was contemporaneous with the journey mentioned in the former clause.

Chapter XVII.

v. 2. neesfū. "*Were gathered together,*" i.e. *during the same time, in which the Philistines were gathering their hosts together.*

v. 10. wĕ-nillāχămāh. "*And let us fight.*"

v. 35. wĕ-yāṣāθī. Here the *wĕ* expresses a close and immediate connexion—"*When the lion came and took a lamb, immediately I went out after him.*"

Chapter XX.

vv. 5-6. The fifth verse is a proposal or suggestion of a course to be taken on the morrow. "*Behold to-morrow is the new moon, and I shall,* etc. *Then thou shalt send me away—And if thy father miss me, then shalt thou say,*" etc,

Chapter XXII.

v. 14. The so-called participle sār, in v. 14, means *one that goeth habitually at any time* at thy bidding.

Chapter XXV.

v. 31. wĕ-hēṭīv Y.—wĕ-zākartā. "And when the Lord dealeth well with thee—then thou shalt remember me."

Chapter XXXI.

v. 10. "And they fastened his body to the wall of Beth-shan" (wĕ—tā*k*eū), *i.e.* during the time in which some were putting his armour in the house of Ashtaroθ, others fastened his body to the wall.

II. Samuel—Chapter I.

v. 1. wai-yēsev. "*Then David abode.*"

Chapter III.

v. 21. ā*k*ūmāh wĕ-ēlēkāh. "*Let me arise and go and let me gather together.*"

v. 24. wai-yēlek halok. i.e. "*And is actually continuing his journey,*" whereas he should have been seized and slain.

v. 39. yesallēm Y. "*May the Lord reward.*"

Chapter VII.

v. 6. wā-ehyeh miθhallēk bĕ-ōhel. "*So that I continue in the state of one who travelleth in a tent.*"

v. 10. wĕ-śamtī. "*And I appointed a place for my children Israel, and planted them.*" These clauses are parts of an enumeration of facts which begins with akriθāh in v. 9, and is carried forward by means of subjoined Perfects into this verse, ending with sākan.

Chapter IX.

vv. 9-10. "All that belonged to Saul I give to thy master's son, and thou art tiller of the land for him, and bringest in the fruits," *i.e.* "And, it being so given, it is thy duty to till the land."

Chapter X.

v. 18. wĕ-ēθ *S.* — hikkāh. *i.e.* "He smote Shorak, *while the general slaughter was still going on.*" To show this, the sequence is broken.

Chapter XI.

v. 15. "*Set ye Uriah in the forefront, and retire ye from him. If ye do so, he will be smitten and die.*" The words wĕ-nikkāh depending on an implied or tacit supposition.

Chapter XII.

The *preface* of Nathan's parable ends with *k*ūnāh. The *narrative* then commences and runs on thus, literally, "*So he nourisheth it, and it groweth up*—of his own food it *eateth*, of his own cup it *drinketh*, in his bosom it *lieth*, and it *becometh* to him as a daughter."

Chapter XIII.'

v. 34. Here, and in v. 37, the English Version uses the same words. In the Hebrew the form varies. In v. 34 the fact of Absalom's flight being there narrated in its proper place, the Imperfect form with *wa* (wai-yivraχ) is used. In v. 37, and again in v. 38, where the writer looks back to this fact from a later point of the story, the form appropriated for marking a breach of sequence is employed, viz. we-A. bāraχ.

Chapter XIV.

v. 7. wĕ-nasmīdāh. Lit. "*And let us destroy the heir also : which if they do, then will they quench my coal which is left.*"

v. 26. kī kāvēd—wĕ-gilliχ-ō. " *When* (in case) *it was heavy on him, then he polled it.*"

v. 28. " *So Absalom dwelt two years in Jerusalem, and saw not the King's face,*" *i.e.* without seeing the King's face during that time. The Perfect rāāh being used, not to indicate a new fact, but to explain the circumstances of the fact just mentioned.

Chapter XVI.

v. 15. wĕ-A. bāū. *i.e.* They had come to Jerusalem whilst the events just narrated were going on.

Chapter XVII.

vv. 1-3. wĕ-ākumāh wĕ-erdĕfāh—wĕ-āvō—wĕ-haχăradtī —wĕ-nās—wē-hikkēθī—wĕ-asīvāh. " *And let me arise and pursue—that I may come upon him while he is weary: if that be done, then shall I make him afraid, and all the people shall flee, and I shall smite the King only. So let me bring back all the people unto thee.*"

v. 17. wĕ-hālĕkāh. This verse states the customary mode of communication. " *The girl used to go and tell them : and they, on receiving any message, immediately started and told the King.*"

v. 18. wai-yar. " *Then,* on the occasion of Hushai's message being forwarded, *a lad saw them.*"

v. 24. " *At the time when David was come to M., Absalom passed over Jordan.*"

v. 25. This verse is a parenthesis. " *Now Absalom had made Amasa captain of the host.*"

CHAPTER XX.

v. 10. wĕ-Yōāb. In this latter part of v. 10 there occurs a breach of sequence. The narrator pauses, to tell what happened between the inflicting of the mortal stroke and the death of Amasa.

CHAPTER XXI.

v. 3. ū-vārăkū. Lit. " *Then bless ye the Lord.*"

I. KINGS—CHAPTER II.

v. 2. ānōkī hōlēk—wĕ-χāzaktā. The death of David will create an immediate necessity for vigorous and decisive action on the part of Solomon.

CHAPTER III.

vv. 7-9. The latter part of v. 7 and the whole of v. 8 are a parenthesis. The direct structure is resumed in v. 9. " *Thou hast made Thy servant king over Thy people—give therefore unto Thy servant an understanding heart to judge Thy people,*" i.e. "Thou didst call him to the office of king and judge; give him therefore the gifts needed for discharging the duties of that office." These two things, the power and the wisdom to use that power aright, should concur. Therefore the structure appropriate to concurrent acts is resorted to (hīmlaktā—wĕ-nāθattā).

CHAPTER VIII.

v. 16. wā-evχar. " *Then, at the end of that time,* during which there had been no place fixed on for a house, *I chose David.*"

v. 27 is a parenthesis. fānīθā, in the beginning of

v. 28, is a Perfect subjoined to the Precative form
yēāmēnnā in v. 26. "*Let Thy word be verified—and have
Thou respect unto the prayer of Thy servant.*" Again at the
beginning of v. 30 is a further subjoined Perfect sāmaɾtā.

v. 32. wĕ-attah tismaɾ. "*Then hear Thou.*" The same
precative form recurs in vv. 34, 36, 39, and 43. In this
verse, and again in v. 49, we have a different construction,
viz. two Perfects used to indicate concurrence or close
connexion : wĕ-sāmaɾtā—wĕ-ɾāśīθā. Lit. "*Thou (who art
a God that keepeth covenant and mercy,* v. 23) *so soon as
Thou hearest the prayer of Thy people, Thou wilt maintain their
cause.*" The mercifulness of God is viewed as necessarily
binding together the prayer of the people and the succour
from their God.

Chapter IX.

v. 25. we-heɾĕleh. The Perfect is here used to express,
not a fact occurring at a certain point of time, but a custom
or fixed practice.

Chapter XIII.

vv. 1-3. "*And behold, whilst Jeroboam was doing the thing
just narrated, a man of God was come from Judah—and
Jeroboam was standing by the altar. Then cried he against
the altar, and said—And he gave a sign*" (wai-yomer—we-
nāθan). The man was engaged in a transaction, which
consisted of two parts : first he announced the woe to
come ; and then he gave a sign to show that, what he
announced, would certainly come to pass. The Imperfect
with *wa* indicates the former part ; the latter part is indicated by a subjoined Perfect.

Chapter XVI.

v. 21. "Then *were* the people *divided* into two parts: half *followed*—and half *followed*." In the former clause, which states a new fact, the Imperfect is used: in the latter clause, which *explains* the former, the Perfect is used (yē̆χālēk—hāyāh aχă̆rē). Compare xviii. 6.

Chapter XX.

v. 33. wĕ-ha-ănāsīm. "*Now the men,* while the king was speaking, *were diligently observing whether anything would come from him. Then,* when he had spoken, they *did hastily catch it.*"

Chapter XXI.

vv. 23-24. In these two verses the words of the E. V., "The dogs shall eat," occur twice. In the former they correspond to the Hebrew words hak-kĕlāvīm yōkĕlū, which are placed in the order usual in such cases. In the latter the sentence being inverted (*i.e.* the object of the verb being put before the verb), these words also are inverted, thus yōkĕlū hak-kelāvīm.

Chapter XXII.

v. 43. "*And he walked* in all the way of Asa his father, he *turned not aside*—from it" (wai-yēlek—lō sūr). The Perfect being used to explain the former verb, much as we might use an adverb or adverbial clause, e.g. *uninterruptedly, without swerving.*

II. Kings—Chapter II.

v. 25. "*And he* (Elisha) *went from thence* to Mount

Carmel. *And from thence he returned* to Samaria " (wai-yēlek—ū-missām sāv). If the journey from Bethel to Carmel had been viewed as distinct from the journey from Carmel to Samaria, we should have had in the latter clause wai-yāsov. But the whole is regarded as one journey. It is therefore to be understood that the prophet's home at that time (or at least the end of his journey) was in Samaria. There is something unusual here in the insertion of two words between the Particle and the Perfect: the insertion however in this case does not express anything more than would have been understood without it.

CHAPTER IV.

v. 22. "*And let me run*" (wĕ-ārūṣāh).

CHAPTER V.

vv. 24-25. wai-yēlēkū—wŏ-hū vā. *i.e.* While the men were on their way back to their master, Gehazi went in and then stood before his master.

CHAPTER IX.

vv. 6-7. *Lit.* "I (the Lord) *anoint thee king—and thou smitest*" (mesaχtī — wĕ-hikkīθā). The two facts being treated as concurrent or immediately connected: the duty of the new king to fulfil the purpose of Him, who gave him the kingship, being apparent.

CHAPTER X.

vv. 2-3. "*Now, seeing your master's sons are with you — look out the best — and fight for your master's house.*" In these verses we find the principle, though not the usual form, of the construction used for marking the concurrence of facts. There is not as usual a Perfect form in both clauses; but v. 2 sets forth certain facts, out of which the fitness of the conduct suggested in the next verse becomes apparent.

CHAPTER XII.

v. 10. wĕ-nāθĕnū. *i.e.* The *custom* was, that the priests put therein all the money that was brought into the house.

CHAPTER XIV.

v. 22. hū bānāh, i.e. *It was he who built.* So likewise the hū is emphatic in v. 25; and again in xv. 35.

CHAPTER XV.

v. 20. "So the king of Assyria *turned back, and stayed not there*" (lō-ʿāmad). The Perfect being used to indicate, not a new fact, but a circumstance connected with the fact last mentioned.

CHAPTER XIX.

v. 24. i.e. "*Whenever I besiege any place,* I dry up the rivers thereof" (wĕ-aχărīv).

CHAPTER XXV.

v. 14. ăser yĕsārĕθū b-ām, i.e. "*Wherewith from time to time they ministered.*"

THE PSALMS.

These Notes refer throughout to the Bible version. The numbers of the verses follow those of the Hebrew text. It will be understood that the renderings, which are occasionally given in these Grammatical Notes of portions of the Hebrew, are not offered as exact and close translations, but rather as paraphrases intended to convey the full meaning of the original.

Psalm I.

v. 3. wĕ-hāyāh. This Perfect is subjoined to the Imperfect in the preceding verse. The result or effect of the meditation is to produce fruit.

Psalm II.

vv. 1-2. The following paraphrase may serve to explain the variations in the forms of the verbs used in these verses :—

"Why are the nations in a *state of rage and uproar* (rāgĕsū) and the people *meditating* a vain design (yehgū) ? Why are the kings *setting themselves* at their posts for battle (yiθyaṣṣĕvū), and why are the rulers *leagued together* against the Lord and against his anointed ?"

v. 4. "*Laugheth—hath them in derision,* even whilst they are defying Him."

v. 5. "*Then speaketh He—and vexeth.*" The Prophet sees all pass before him in vision.

v. 6. wa-ănī. Before Alef *wa* is used for *we.* The pronoun ănī is expressed for the purpose of emphasis. "*Yet I—it is I that have anointed.*"

Psalm III.

v. 8. hikkīθā. "*For Thou smitest—Thou art the smiter of mine enemies—Thou breakest.*"

Psalm V.

v. 12. wĕ-θāsēk. "*And defend Thou them.*" The 2nd

person Imperfect is here shown to be Precative, by being placed in close connexion with Precatives, before and after.

v. 13. "For Thou *dost bless—dost compass,*" *i.e.* dost shield the righteous man from harm, *when (if at any time) it comes nigh him.* This sense is suggested by the Imperfect.

Psalm VI.

v. 10. yi*kkā*χ. "*He receiveth,* is even now receiving, *my prayer.*"

Psalm VII.

v. 5. wā-aχalleṣāh. wū for wa, because of the Alef following. "*If I rewarded evil unto him that was at peace with me—which I did not—nay, rather, I went further, and I delivered—let go free—him that without cause was mine enemy.*"

v. 16. Lit. "*He made a pit and then he digged it deep—and after that he fell.*"

v. 17. yāsūv. "*Let his mischief return upon his own head.*"

Psalm VIII.

v. 6. wat-tĕχassĕrēhū. "*Not only art Thou mindful of him and visitest him,* but then Thy goodness passeth beyond this, Thou *makest him little lower than the angels: Thou makest him to have dominion,*" etc.

Psalm IX.

v. 4. āsīθū—yāsavtū. The Perfects are here used to assert that which is true, not at one time only, but at all times. "*Thou maintainest—Thou sittest.*"

v. 15. āgīlāh. "Let me rejoice."

v. 20. "*Let the nations know.*"

PSALM X.

v. 3. hillēl. The Perfect is used to express a settled habit or character. "*He is a boaster.*"

v. 17. sāmaₜtā. "*Thou ever hearest.*"

PSALM XI.

v. 2. kōněnū. This Perfect is subjoined to the Imperfect yidrěkūn. The two clauses indicate two stages in the preparation to shoot. In prose wě would be prefixed to the Perfect.

PSALM XIII.

vv. 5-6. bātaχtī. "*I trust habitually in thy mercy. Let my heart rejoice. Let me sing unto the Lord,* (i.e. find a subject for song) *in that He hath dealt bountifully with me.*"

PSALM XIV.

v. 1. The Perfect āmar expresses the habitual thought or sentiment of the fool, *i.e.* of the ungodly man.

v. 5. pāχădū. "*All the while they*—the ungodly—*are in a state of great fear, for God,* who gives peace and confidence, *is not with them.*"

PSALM XV.

vv. 2-3. The positive characteristics of the man (who shall dwell on the holy hill) are expressed by the so-called *participle* or *nomen agentis :* the negative, by lō with a Perfect as in Ps. i. v. 1. In both cases alike, *permanent characteristics or habits* are intended.

6

v. 4. yĕkabbēd. "*He honoureth such persons, whenever he meets with them.*" This sense is suggested by the Imperfect.

PSALM XVI.

v. 4. "*Many be their sorrows.*"

v. 7. ăvārek. "*I bless*—I am now blessing." This Psalm is the utterance of the blessing.

v. 10. lō-θaăzōv. "*Thou wilt not leave.*" The reference to Sĕōl implies a future time.

PSALM XVII.

v. 6. ănī-ḱĕrāθī-kā — kī θaănēnī. "*I am a caller*—I call habitually—*upon Thee, because, whenever I call, Thou hearest me.*"

v. 9. yaḱḱīfū. "*Are compassing me about.*"

v. 11. "*They are setting.*"

v. 14. wĕ-hinnīχū. "*And leave.*" This Perfect is subjoined to the Imperfect yisbeᵘū. "*These wealthy men have many children, and leave to them the rest of their substance.*"

v. 15. eśbeᵃāh. "*Let me be filled.*"

PSALM XVIII.

v. 2. erχom-kā. "*I love Thee.*" This Psalm is the expression of my love.

eχseh. "*In whom I take refuge in time of danger.*"

v. 4. ekrā—ū-ivvāsēvaᵃ. "*When I call, I am delivered. So soon as I call, the deliverance comes.*"

vv. 5-6. These verses set forth the state of danger and terror out of which the Psalmist has been delivered.

" *Sorrows are coiled round him like cords, floods of ungodly men are making him afraid, etc. He is crying to God. Then comes the deliverance.*"

vv. 8-20. In these verses the several stages of this deliverance are narrated. " *Then quaketh the earth and trembleth—then boweth He the heavens,*" etc.

v. 21. " *The Lord is rewarding me according to my righteousness, according to, etc., doth He recompense me.*"

vv. 26-7. " *Thou shewest Thyself* merciful," etc.; and so throughout.

vv. 28-9. "*For Thou savest—bringest down—lightest—The Lord enlighteneth,*" etc.

v. 29. "*I run—I leap.*"

v. 36. " *So Thou givest me the shield of Thy salvation, and Thy right hand is holding me up, and Thy gentleness is making me great.*"

v. 37. " Thou *enlargest—and my feet slip not.*"

v. 38. "*When I pursue—I overtake.*"

In all these verses 37-46 the Imperfect is to be rendered as a ∙Present. The Psalmist throughout these verses is thankfully acknowledging the deliverances which God works for him from day to day.

v. 49. " *Thou deliverest me.*"

Psalm XIX.

v. 2. Lit. " *The heavens are tellers* (mĕsapperīm) *of the glory of God, and the firmament is a shewer-forth of His handywork.*" It is the *office* or *function* of the heavens to testify to the greatness of the Creator. This is expressed by the so-called Participle.

v. 3. The transmission of this knowledge, by each day and each night in its turn, is properly expressed by the Imperfect.

Psalm XXI.

v. 1. "*O Lord, in Thy strength doth the King rejoice.*" The position of 'yiśmaχ' before 'melek' is owing to the inversion of the sentence.

v. 6. tĕsavveh. "*Art Thou laying.*"

v. 7. "*For Thou makest him—art now making him.*"

v. 9. "*May thy hand find out all thine enemies,*" *i.e.* May the King, who hath just conquered one enemy, in like manner conquer all. From another part of the quire comes the latter clause of the verse, "*Thy right hand shall find.*"

Psalm XXII.

v. 16. tispeθēnī. "*Thou art bringing me.*"

v. 27. yōkĕlū ảnāwīm. "*Let the meek eat — let them praise*—may your heart live."

v. 28. "*May all — remember and turn — and may all worship before Thee.*"

v. 30. This verse seems to be a response from another part of the quire to the invitation in v. 27. "*They ate, and then they worshipped, even all that be fat in the land. Before his face are bowing all that be gone down to the dust.*" The latter clause is inverted, and therefore the verb comes before its noun or subject.

Psalm XXIII.

v. 1. "*I lack not anything.*"

v. 4. The first clause of this verse imparts a future

time to the whole. "*I will fear no evil, for Thou wilt be with me—they shall comfort me.*"

Psalm XXIV.

v. 2. yĕkōnĕne-hā. "*He is still sustaining it,* or *keeping it firm.*"

Psalm XXV.

3. "*None that wait on Thee shall be ashamed.*" vv. 5-10 are a sort of parenthesis, proceeding from another part of the quire. At v. 11 the former voices resume their chant, repeating in substance the words with which they closed it. Instead of "*for Thy goodness' sake,*" they now say, "for Thy Name's sake." The Perfect salaχtā is subjoined to the Imperative zĕkōr in v. 7.

v. 15. yōṣī. "*Whenever my feet are caught in a net, He plucketh them out.*"

Psalm XXVI.

v. 8. āhavtī. "*I love—I am a lover of.*"

Psalm XXVII.

v. 2. hēmmāh. The pronoun is here expressed for the purpose of emphasis. "*It* was *they, not I,* that stumbled."

v. 4. sāaltī—ōθāh avakkēs. "*One thing I pray for constantly—that thing I am earnestly seeking now.*"

Psalm XXVIII.

v. 1. ekrā. "*Do I cry.*" The Psalm itself is the cry.

v. 6. sāmaᶜ. "*He heareth at all times.*"

v. 7. "*My heart trusteth habitually, with my song do I praise Him.*"

Psalm XXIX.

v. 3. hirʻim. The use of the Perfect shows that the stress is on the act, not on the time. "*It is the God of Glory that thundereth.*"

v. 8. histartī—hāyīθī. Concurrent Perfects. "*So soon as Thou didst hide Thy face, I was troubled.*"

v. 9. "*In my trouble I cried.*" The cry or supplication is expressed in vv. 10-11.

Psalm XXXI.

v. 7. "*I hate.*"

v. 8. āgīlāh. "*Let me be glad and rejoice in Thy mercy, for that Thou considerest my trouble.*"

v. 12. hayīθi. "*I am become a reproach*, etc. *They that see me, flee from me.*" These words do not refer to any particular act, but to the ordinary conduct, of the Psalmist's friends. Therefore the Perfect is used.

Psalm XXXII.

v. 7. "*Thou preservest me. Thou compassest me.*"

v. 8. A voice from another part of the quire is heard saying, "*I am instructing thee*, etc.—*I am guiding thee.*"

Psalm XXXIV.

vv. 5-6. dārastī—wĕ-ʻānā-nī. "*Whenever—so soon as— I seek, He answers me.*"

A similar construction occurs in v. 6, "*When they look, they are enlightened.*" Then comes a voice from another part of the quire, "*So be it ever—May they never look in vain;*" or, according to the Hebrew idiom, "*May their faces never be ashamed.*"

v. 19. yoṣiaᵣ. The Imperfect is here used to state, not the existence of a specific fact, but that a certain fact always recurs under certain conditions, " *If men be of a contrite spirit, He saveth them.*"

Psalm XXXV.

v. 11. A pause is to be made after yĕkūmūn. " *They stand up as witnesses,*" etc.

v. 13. tāsūv. " *Returneth.*"

v. 15. śamĕχū. " *They are glad, and are gathered together—They tear* (or *revile*) *me and cease not.*"

vv. 20-21. wai-yarχīvū. "*From secret plotting they proceed to open denunciation.*"

Psalm XXXVI.

v. 13. " *Are not able.*"

Psalm XXXVII.

v. 3. sĕkōn. " *Dwell* (abide) *in the land and feed in safety.*"

v. 6. The Perfect hōṣī is *subjoined* to yaᵣāśeh in the preceding verse.

v. 11. hiθᵣannĕgū. This Perfect is subjoined to the Imperfect yīrĕsū.

v. 13. yiśχak. "*Laugheth—is laughing, whilst the wicked man is plotting.*"

v. 40. wai-yaᵣzĕrēm. "*Then, when trouble has befallen them, the Lord helpeth them and delivereth—delivereth them from the wicked, and saveth them.*"

Psalm XXXVIII.

v. 2. wat-tinχaθ. " *First come Thy arrows from a dis-*

tance; then Thy hand, which shot the arrows, presseth me sore."

v. 12. ōhavai.   *"Even my personal friends are now beginning to take the position, which my kinsfolk habitually take."*

v. 13. wa-inaksū.   *"Others, seeing this, become actively hostile."*

v. 14. wa-ĕhī.   *"So I become as a man that heareth not."*

v. 16. ūmartī.   *"I think—this is my constant thought— Thou wilt hear me, lest,"* etc.

v. 19. aggīd—edag.   *"I declare—I am sorry."*   The Psalm itself being the utterance of the Psalmist's confession and sorrow.

PSALM XXXIX.

v. 2. ūmartī.   *"I say habitually, Let me take heed—let me keep."*

vv. 3-4.   *"I am dumb—I hold my peace—my sorrow is stirred.   My heart is hot within me : While I am musing a fire is burning.   I speak, am speaking, with my tongue."*

This is not a narration of a sequence of facts.   If so, we should have found ' wā-ădabbēr.'   Rather, it is a description of an inward conflict, in the course of which the habitual purpose to keep silence is not abandoned and voluntarily followed by speech, but simply overborne (while still subsisting) by the force of strong and bitter feelings.   As if the Psalmist had said, *" The settled resolve of my mind is to abstain from speaking, lest I sin in speaking. My state is that of a dumb man.   But, all the while, a fire is burning within me.   All unawares, I find myself a speaker. I am forced to utter my distress."*

Psalm XL.

In vv. 2-3 and the former clause of v. 4 the several steps of some past deliverance are recounted in the ordinary narrative form.

v. 4. yirū. "*May many see it and fear and trust in the Lord.*"

v. 8. hinneh, vā𝜃ī. "*Lo, I am come.*" Compare Numb. xxii. 38, II. Sam. xix. 21.

v. 10. biśśartī follows the time of χāfastī in v. 9. "*I proclaim—I am a proclaimer.*" lō-eklā. "*I refrain not my lips from speaking,*" i.e. *whenever a fit time comes.*

v. 12. Attāh lo 𝜃iklū. "*Thou, Lord, wilt not refrain* (withhold) *Thy tender mercies — Thy loving-kindness and Thy truth will continually preserve me.*"

Psalm XLI.

v. 3. wě-al-tittěnēhū. "*And do not Thou deliver him unto the will of his enemies.*" This is a cry of supplication from another part of the quire. Likewise, a direct address to God occurs in the latter clause of v. 4.

v. 5. ănī ūmartī. "*As for me, my constant prayer is.*"

v. 7. yēṣē—yedabbēr. "*As soon as he goeth out of the sick chamber, he begins to utter iniquity.*"

Psalm XLII.

v. 4. ēlleh ezkěrāh. "These things let me remember (kī e𝑐ěvōr) *how from time to time I passed on amidst the multitude of worshippers, even to (𝑐ad) the house of God.*"

The word ēlleh (these) refers to the acts about to be mentioned. Compare Gen. ii. 1.

Psalm XLIII.

v. 4. wĕ-āvōᾱh. *"And let me come unto the altar of God —then upon the harp will I praise Thee."*

Psalm XLIV.

vv. 6-8. nenaggēᾱh. *"Through Thee do we push down— do we tread them under. For I trust not in my bow, neither doth my sword save me. But Thou art our Saviour from our enemies."*

v. 10. wat-taklīm-ēnū. *"So Thou puttest (art putting) us to shame."*

v. 19. lō here negatives the whole of the verse. *"It is not the case that our heart is turned back, and so our steps declined from Thy way."*

v. 20. wan-nifrōś. *"If we have forgotten our own God, and so turned to the worship of false gods."*

Psalm XLV.

v. 1. The words "are inditing" would require an Imperfect, in the Hebrew. The word rāχaś seems to express some strong emotion or fervour.

v. 8. āhavtā—wat-tiśnā. *"Thou art a lover of righteousness, and so Thou hatest wickedness."*

v. 9. *"Kings' daughters are among thy honorable women: upon thy right hand is set the queen."* The Psalmist sees before him the pomp of the royal marriage, and being so present in body or mind, proceeds to address his words to the bride in vv. 11-12. Then vv. 13-16 set forth the splendour of the marriage procession.

v. 13. *"And the daughter of Tyre is there with a gift— even the rich among the people intreat thy favour."*

v. 15. tūval. "*She is (now) led*"—the procession is moving on.

vv. 15-16. "*Are they brought—they are entering.*"

vv. 17-18. A second address to the bride.

Psalm XLVI.

v. 4. Lit. "*Let the waters thereof roar—let the mountains shake—*(yet is there) *a river, the streams whereof make (are making) glad the city of God.*"

v. 6. "*He shall help her, even God.*"

v. 10. In the second clause of this verse *kişēş* is a Perfect subjoined to the Imperfect yesabbēr. The destruction of the weapons of war is regarded as one operation.

Psalm XLVII.

vv. 3-4. "*He subdueth—is subduing.—He chooseth.*"

Psalm XLVIII.

v. 10. dīmmīnū. "*We think habitually upon—we reflect upon.*"

Psalm XLIX.

v. 11. wĕ-ɑzĕvū is a Perfect subjoined to the Imperfect yōvēdū.

v. 15. "*Death feedeth on them : then have the upright dominion over them.*"

Psalm L.

v. 3. yāvō. "*Let God come, and let Him not keep silence.*" This clause comes from another part of the quire. It expresses the longing of godly men for the manifestation of God's righteous government of the world. In the following words the narrative is resumed: "*A fire devoureth before him, and it is very tempestuous*" etc.

v. 4. "*He calleth.*"

v. 6. wai-yaggīdū. "*Then (thereupon) the heavens declare His righteousness.*" This is the response, or joyful acclaim, of the heavens to the divine call in v. 4.

vv. 16-17. wal-tiśśā berīθ-ī. "*Thou presumest not only to declare (recount) my statutes, professing knowledge of them, but to go further and acknowledge a personal obligation to obedience: whereas all the time thou art a hater (śānēθā) of instruction, and from hatred proceedest even to open rejection of the Divine commands*" (wat-taslēk).

Psalm LI.

v. 8 (E. V. 6). θōdī‹ēnī. "Thou makest, *art making, me to know.*"

Psalm LII.

v. 9 (E. V. 7). wai-yivtaχ. "*And so (for man must have something to trust in) begins to trust in his wealth, and to make a god of that.*"

Psalm LIII.

v. 5. ōkĕlē—ākĕlū. *Lit.* being eaters of my people, they are eaters of bread, i.e. "*Eating up my people is to them as natural and habitual as eating bread.*"

Psalm LIV.

v. 7 (E.V. 5). yāsīv. "*He is rewarding.*" The Psalmist, seeing this, prays for the utter discomfiture of the oppressors.

Psalm LV.

v. 6 (E.V. 5). yāvō. "*Come upon me (assail me)*— wat-tekass-ēnī, *then, as a further stage of distress, horror overwhelms me.*"

v. 7. wā-ōmar. *"Then I say."* This horror prevails to such a degree as to force from me these words, " *O that I had wings like a dove—Let me flee away and be at rest."*

v. 10. raīθī. *"I see habitually, I witness."*

vv. 12-13. *"For it is not an enemy that reproacheth me : then could I bear it : neither is it he that hated me that hath magnified himself against me. But it is thou."*

v. 18. pūdāh. *"He redeemeth—He is the redeemer—for there are many with me."*

v. 20. yismaₑ El. *"May God hear."*

v. 21. sūlaχ. *"He puts forth his hand habitually—he breaks (is a breaker of) his covenant."* So likewise throughout v. 22.

Psalm LVII.

vv. 2-3. eχĕseh. *"Do I make—am I now making—my refuge—I cry."*

v. 4. yislaχ. *"May He send from heaven—May God send forth."*

Psalm LVIII.

v. 11. yiśmaχ ṣaddīk. *"Let the righteous man rejoice— his feet let him wash."*

Psalm LIX.

v. 9. tiśχak. *"Whilst they are so daring and scornful, Thou all the time hast them in derision."*

vv. 15-17. *" They return—they wander. Then they grudge. But I sing."* The pronoun, ănī, being expressed for the sake of contrast.

Psalm LX.

v. 6 (E. V. 4). This verse is identical in structure with

the preceding verses ; yet whilst those verses speak only
of distress and terror, this seems to speak of some hopeful
sign following on past hopelessness. If this be the meaning, this verse would regularly be introduced by *wa* with
an Imperfect. One way presents itself of escaping from
this difficulty, namely to regard the latter clause of v. 3,
and the whole of v. 6, as proceeding from a different voice
or different part of the quire. The three petitions which
thus mingle with the words of sorrow and complaint, are
these—"*Mayest Thou return to us again—Heal Thou the past
—Encourage Thou us for the future.*" In this view the Perfect nāθattū at the beginning of v. 6 is subjoined to the
Imperative rĕfāh in v. 4, the *we* which in prose would be
prefixed to it being omitted. The Particle *we* is not
needed, because the connexion is sufficiently indicated by
the recurrence of the chant from the same part of the
quire. ·"*Gilead shall be mine.*" *Shall be* should be substituted for *is* throughout the sentence.

v. 12. Rather perhaps, "*Wilt not Thou, O God ?* Hast
Thou cast us off and goest not forth with our armies ?"
(zenaχtā-nū wĕ-lo-ṣēṣē). "Hast Thou so entirely cast us
off, that Thou wilt not go forth with our armies ?"

Psalm LXIII.

v. 1. "*Early do I seek Thee.*"

Psalm LXIV.

v. 8. wai-yōr-ēm. This verse refers to v. 5. "*Suddenly
do they shoot their arrows. Then the arrow of God strikes
them—suddenly are they wounded.*"

vv. 9-10. "*So they make their own tongue to* etc.—*All that see them flee away—Then all men fear—for they wisely consider.*"

v. 11. "*Let the righteous be glad in the Lord and trust in Him—and let the upright in heart glory.*"

Psalm LXV.

v. 2 (E.V. 1). yĕsūllam. "*Unto Thee is the vow of each man performed.*"

v. 3. sōmēa‹ tĕfillāh. Lit. "*Hearer of prayer, even unto Thee do all men come,*" i.e. Thou hearest prayer, not at any particular time, but at all times: wherefore all come unto Thee, knowing that Thou hearest all. (yāvōū). "*They come from time to time, whenever they are in sorrow or trouble.*"

v. 4. Attāh θekappĕrēm. The pronoun is expressed for the *purpose* of emphasis or contrast. "*Thou—Thou only, purgest them away.*"

v. 6. ta‹ānēnū. "*By terrible things dost Thou answer us, when we pray.*"

v. 9. wai-yīrĕū. "So *they that dwell* etc., *fear.*"

Psalm LXVI.

v. 12. "*Thou didst cause men to ride over our heads; we went through fire and through water, then Thou broughtest us out.*"

Psalm LXVII.

v. 5. kī θispōt. "*For that Thou judgest—and governest.*"

vv. 7-8. nattenāh. "*The earth hath yielded her increase. May God, our own God, continue to bless us—May God bless us, and may all the ends of the earth fear him.*"

Psalm LXVIII.

v. 8. rā.āsāh. "*Shook.*" The Past time is indicated by the words bĕ-ṣc̄θĕkū.

v. 10. Here gesem and naχ̆ălāθĕ-kū may be regarded as equivalent to a double accusative after a verb of motion. The latter clause is a case of Concurrent Perfects; as if it were written wĕ-nilāh—wĕ-kōnantā. But the necessity of introducing the emphatic Attāh has led to the omission of the second *wĕ*; which if introduced must have been prefixed to the verb, and so would have broken the connexion of the pronoun Attāh with its verb. "*A plenteous rain wast Thou all the time sending upon Thine inheritance. Whenever it was weary, Thou didst confirm it.*"

v. 14. im-tiskevūn. This may be regarded as a strong negative, "*Ye shall never lie,*" as in Ps. xcv. 11.

v. 23. āmar. It is the *purpose* or *decree* of God to bring his people from the lands wherein they are scattered, back again to this land; even from the Eastern mountains, even from the Western sea.

v. 25. The Psalmist, after reviewing the history of his people from their passage through the desert to their establishment in the land, dwells now on the crowning mercy of God who had enabled them to be habitual witnesses of the stately worship of Jerusalem. rāū. "*They see,*" i.e. regularly, and as a custom.

v. 26. kiddĕmū. The Perfect indicates the established order of the processions in the holy place. "*The singers go before—The players on instruments follow after—among them are*" etc.

v. 32. yĕĕθāyū. "*May princes come out of Egypt—Even Ethopia—may she stretch out soon her hands unto God.*"

Psalm LXIX.

vv. 11-12. wā-evkeh—wā-ettĕnāh. "*So I wept—Then I made sackcloth my garment.*"

Psalm LXXI.

v. 24. kī-vōsū. "*For that they are confounded:*" or, *when they are confounded.* The confusion of his enemies will be the evidence of the righteous judgment of God.

Psalm LXXII.

v. 2. yādīn. A Precative Form: one in the series of petitions which commences with 'tēn' in the first verse, and is carried on by 'yiśū hārīm' in v. 3, and so on from verse to verse as far v. 8.

vv. 9-15. These verses are to be taken as indicative or affirmative. The sentence in v. 9 being inverted, and v. 10 following the time of v. 9. This whole passage is a response from another part of the quire, expressing an assurance that the prayer just heard will be more than fulfilled.

vv. 16-17. The whole of v. 16, and the first clause of v. 17, "*May his name endure for ever,*" etc., are precative. The latter part of v. 17 is a response, as before.

Psalm LXXIII.

v. 3. ereh. Imperfect. "*Whilst I was beholding—witnessing —the prosperity of the wicked.*"

v. 13. wā-erχas̩. Lit. "*So, or then, I wash,*" i.e. purity

7

dwelling in the heart, extends itself to the hands—to all the acts and doings of the man.

v. 14. wā-ĕhī. *"Then I become,"* i.e. after all this striving to be just and holy, pain and sorrow follow.

v. 15. āmartī—bāgadtī. Every such thought is an offence, an act of disloyalty.

v. 18. tāsīθ. *"Whilst I am envying and marvelling, Thou settest them up and castest them down."* 'hippaltā' is a Perfect subjoined to the Imperfect tāsīθ; the *wĕ*, which would have been prefixed in prose to the Perfect, being here omitted.

vv. 21-22. kī yiθχammēṣ. *"Though my heart is grieved, and I am etc.—So foolish am I—I am as a beast before Thee—Nevertheless—."*

Psalm LXXIV.

v. 5. yivvādaʿ. *"Formerly a man became famous for hewing down the trees of the forest, wherewith to make carved work, But now—."*

v. 8. āmĕrū. *"They say in their heart, i.e. their deliberate thought, or purpose, is—."*

Psalm LXXV.

v. 8. sōfēt—yaspīl—yārīm. Here the Participle or *nomen agentis* expresses the office, the general and permanent character; whilst the Imperfects express the special acts, by which from time to time that character is manifested.

Psalm LXXVI.

vv. 2-3. wa-ihī. *"After the knowledge of God had been*

established in the land, then Salem became the seat of His worship."

v. 11. tōde-kā—taχgōr. *"The wrath of man praiseth Thee, i.e. yieldeth cause for praise—dost Thou restrain."*

v. 13. yivṣōr. *"Cutteth off—represseth."*

Psalm LXXVII.

v. wĕ-haʿazīn. *"And (for) he giveth ear to me at all times."*

v. 13. wĕ-hāgīθī. *"And meditate."* This Perfect is subjoined to the Imperfect ezkĕrāh, as marking a further stage of the same proceeding. But in the next clause the wĕ (ū) is prefixed to the noun; so the verb reverts to its original form as an Imperfect.

v. 16. *"Thou didst redeem."*

v. 19. *"In the sea was Thy way—and Thy footsteps were not known."*

Psalm LXXVIII.

v. 5. wai-yākem. *"Then, after those wonderful works wrought in the delivery of the people out of bondage, He appointed a law."*

Psalm LXXX.

v. 16. yōvēdū. *"At the rebuke of thy countenance, they (Thy people) are perishing."*

Psalm LXXXII.

v. 1. yispōt. *"Is judging."*

v. 5. lō yādĕʿū — wĕ-lō yāvīnū. Here the Perfect is used to express a permanent fact—a state of gross ignorance. The inability to discern between the just and the unjust, in particular cases, is expressed by the Imperfect.

Psalm LXXXIII.

v. 3. ya*a*rīmū. *"They are taking—are consulting."*

Psalm LXXXIV.

v. 4. *"They (or who) are continually praising Thee."*

Psalm LXXXV.

vv. 2-4. These verses set forth, by the use of a series of Perfects, the abiding character or attributes of the God of Israel. He is a God who is favourable to His land—who brings His people back from captivity—who forgives iniquity and covers sin—who takes away wrath, and turns Himself from the fierceness of His anger. Upon this follows vv. 5-6 the prayer that God will turn His people from their offences (their *folly* mentioned in v. 8), so that His wrath, from which they are suffering at the time, may cease.

v. 8. esmĕ*a*āh. *"Let me hear what God the Lord is speaking—for He is speaking peace unto His people—but let them not turn again to folly."*

v. 12. *"Springeth—is springing—looks down constantly."*

vv. 13-14. A continued description of a present blessing—*giveth—yieldeth—goeth—setteth* (or *is setting*).

Psalm LXXXVIII.

v. 14. sivva*a*tī—θĕkaddĕme-kā. *"Unto Thee, do I cry at all times. Even at the first break of day, doth my prayer come before Thee."*

v. 17. sabbūnī. "*They surround me, like water, all the day; they compass me about together.*"

Psalm LXXXIX.

v. 3. āmartī. "*I say—this is my settled and habitual conviction: to which I still hold fast, notwithstanding the perplexity and trouble of the time.*"

vv. 4-5. In these verses the Psalmist cites the Divine promise, on which his conviction rests.

v. 5. akīn—ū-vānīθū. The Imperfect and the Perfect subjoined to it, express two stages of one process; the laying of the foundation, and the rearing of the fabric.

vv. 12-17. A present time runs through these verses. The word 'shall' ought to be omitted wherever it occurs in them.

Psalm XC.

v. 2. bĕ-ṭerem — wat-tĕχōlēl. "*Before the mountains were brought forth and, when after the close of that period, Thou didst form the earth (or cause the earth to bring forth).*" With the structure of this verse compare the structure of Ps. xcii. 8.

Psalm XCI.

v. 7. yippōl elēf. Lit. "*Let a thousand fall,*" i.e. *if a thousand fall.* Compare Ps. cxxxix. 18.

v. 15. yikrā. "*As soon as he calls, I will answer him.*"

Psalm XCII.

v. 5. "*I triumph.*" In this Psalm I am expressing my triumphant gladness.

v. 10. yōvēdū — yiθpārĕdū. "*Are perishing — are*

scattered." This (as shown by hinnēh) is the present fact in which the Psalmist is triumphing.

v. 11. *Then, after the destruction of mine enemies, Thou exaltest me.*

v. 12. *"So mine eye seeth."* A present time runs through the remainder of the Psalm.

Psalm XCIII.

vv. 3-4. yiśū. *"Let the floods lift up their waves—yet than the noise of many waters the Lord on high is mightier."*

Psalm XCIV.

v. 7. The word *doth* should be substituted for *shall* in this verse; and likewise in vv. 9-10.

vv. 22-23. wa-ihī Y. *" Then, at that stage of wickedness, the Lord is my defence. So He bringeth upon them their own iniquity, and cutteth them off."*

Psalm XCVI.

v. 13. kī vā. *"For He is come—He is come to judge."* Compare v. 10, mālak. *"He is already King."*

Psalm XCVII.

v. 10. sōmēr—yaṣṣīl. "He is their keeper, their guardian, *at all times.* He delivereth them out of the hand of the wicked, *whenever* the wicked assail them."

Psalm CII.

v. 17. kī vānāh. *"When the Lord hath built up Zion, and hath appeared in His glory."*

v. 18. The particle kī is carried on to this verse, *" (When) He hath regarded the prayer of the destitute, and not despised their prayer."*

v. 19. tikkāθēv zōθ. *"Let this be written."*

v. 20. *"When He hath looked down, when the Lord from heaven hath beheld the earth."*

vv. 24-25. *wa* is omitted before ōmar. *" So I said."*

Psalm CIV.

v. 12. *"By them the fowls of the heaven have their habitation."*

v. 31. yĕhī kĕvōd. *" Be the glory of the Lord for ever. May the Lord rejoice in His work."*

Psalm CVI.

v. 17. tiftaχ. In a prose narrative a *wa* would have been prefixed to the verb, thus wat-tiftaχ.

v. 34. lō-hismīdū. This verse serves as a Preface to the narrative following in vv. 35-42, which sets forth the events which sprang out of the fact stated in the Preface.

v. 48. wĕ-āmar. This is a kind of rubric concerning the use of the preceding words of blessing, with which this Fourth Book of the Psalms closes. *"When the reader recites these words, then shall all the people say, Amen."* This was the established form for this purpose. See Deut. xxvii. 16-26.

Psalm CVII.

v. 24. hemmāh rāū. *" These men are habitually witnesses of the works of the Lord in the deep."* Compare Ps. lxviii. 25.

Psalm CVIII.

This Psalm is composed of parts of two earlier Psalms, viz. Ps. lvii. 7-11, and Ps. lx. 5-12.

Psalm CIX.

v. 16. wai-yardōf. "Not only did he show no mercy, *but he went further and persecuted the poor."*

v. 25. wa-ănī hāyīθī. *"And I am become a reproach unto them—when they look upon me, they shake their heads."*

v. 28. *"Let them curse—for Thou art blessing me all the while. They rise up against me. Then are they ashamed, but Thy servant rejoiceth."*

Psalm CX.

v. 3. lĕ-kā. *"Thou shalt have."*

v. 4. Attāh kōhēn. The promise, at the time of making it, is confirmed by an oath; but the fulfilment is future. *"Thou shalt be a priest for ever."*

v. 5. The difficulty, which has perplexed the expounders of this verse, may be removed by a small change in the stops; namely, by placing a comma after Adōnāi, and cancelling the Masoretic stop after yĕmīn-kā. The passage will then run thus: *"O Lord, at Thy right hand did he (my Lord) smite kings in the day of his wrath."*

v. 6. yādīn. *"He judgeth (is executing judgment) among the nations: he hath filled—he hath smitten."*

v. 7. *"From a brook in the way he drinketh,"* i.e. in his pursuit of the defeated enemies. *"Therefore he lifts up his head,"* i.e. is refreshed and follows on, till he has utterly subdued them, according to the promise in v. 1.

Thus, the promise is set forth in vv. 1-4: the fulfilment is described in vv. 5-7.

Psalm CXV.

v. 2. yōmĕrū. "*Wherefore say the heathen ?*"

v. 12. Y. zĕkār-ānū. "*The Lord is mindful of us.*"

v. 14. yōsēf Y. "*The Lord increase you.*"

Psalm CXVIII.

v. 27. El Y. wai-yāēr. "*The Lord is God—so He sheweth light.*"

Psalm CXIX.

v. 40. tāavtī. "*I long—I am in an abiding or habitual state of longing.*" This force of the Perfect is recognized in v. 42, but not in vv. 43, 47, 48, and other places.

v. 171. tabbaᵣnāh śĕfāθai. "*Let my lips utter praise, when Thou teachest me Thy statutes.*"

v. 172. "*Let my tongue speak (sing).*"

Psalm CXXI.

v. 1. "*I lift up.*"

vv. 3-4. al-yittēn. "*May He not suffer thy foot to be moved: May He not slumber that keepeth thee. Behold, neither slumbereth nor sleepeth He that keepeth Israel.*"

Psalm CXXII.

v. 2. "*Our feet stand,*" lit. *have become standers* (ōmĕdōθ hāyū).

v. 3. "Jerusalem, *that is now builded,* is as a city that is compact together" (hab-bĕnūyāh).

v. 4. ᵃālū. "*Go up,*" i.e. as a custom regularly observed. Compare I. Sam. i. 3.

v. 6. "*May they prosper that love Thee.*"

¶   Psalm CXXVIII.

vv. 5-6. "*The Lord bless thee out of Zion, and see thou the good of Jerusalem—and see thou thy children's children.*"

Psalm CXXX.

v. 1. kĕrāθī-kā. "*Do I cry unto Thee.*"

Psalm CXXXII.

v. 7. nāvōāh. "*Let us go.*"

v. 9. kōhăne-kā. "*Then, when Thou arisest, shall thy priests be clothed with righteousness and Thy saints shall shout for joy.*"

Psalm CXXXVI.

v. 21. This Perfect nāθan is subjoined to the Imperfect yahărōg in v. 18.

Psalm CXXXVIII.

v. 4. "*May all the kings praise Thee.*"

Psalm CXXXIX.

v. 1. χakarta-nī wat-tēdāɛ. Lit. "*Thou penetratest—pervadest me at all times—and so Thou knowest.*"

v. 13. "*Thou didst possess—Thou wast covering me.*" The noun suggests the notion of past time.

Psalm CXLII.

v. 2. "*I cry unto the Lord—unto the Lord do I make my supplication.*" All these verses 2-5 describe a *present* state of distress, which moves the Psalmist to the prayer contained in vv. 6-8.

v. 6. zāɛakti—ūmarti. "*I cry habitually—I say,*" i.e. *it is my settled thought—my conviction.*

Psalm CXLIII.

v. 7. wĕ-nimsaltī. "*Hide not Thy face from me. If Thou hide Thy face, then shall I be made like unto them that go down into the grave.*"

Psalm CXLIV.

v. 3. wat-tēda·ēhū. "What is man, *so that, in consequence whereof, Thou takest knowledge of him?*"

Psalm CXLVI.

v. 10. yimlōk. "*Be the Lord king.*"

Psalm CXLVIII.

v. 14. wai-yārem. "*So,* being such, *He exalteth.*"

STEPHEN AUSTIN AND SONS, PRINTERS, HERTFORD.